Cram101 Textbook Outlines to accompany:

Business Statistics: Contemporary Decision Making

Ken Black, 6th Edition

A Content Technologies Inc. publication (c) 2010.

Cram101 Textbook Outlines and Cram101.com are Cram101 Inc. publications and services. All notes, highlights, reviews, and practice tests are written and prepared by Content Technologies and Cram101, all rights reserved.

WHY STOP HERE... THERE'S MORE ONLINE

With technology and experience, we've developed tools that make studying easier and efficient. Like this Cram101 textbook notebook, **Cram101.com** offers you the highlights from every chapter of your actual textbook. However, unlike this notebook, **Cram101.com** gives you practice tests for each of the chapters. You also get access to in-depth reference material for writing essays and papers.

By purchasing this book, you get 50% off the normal subscription free!. Just enter the promotional code **'DK73DW12197'** on the Cram101.com registration screen.

CRAMI01.COM FEATURES:

Outlines & Highlights
Just like the ones in this notebook, but with links to additional information.

Integrated Note Taking
Add your class notes to the Cram101 notes, print them and maximize your study time.

Problem Solving
Step-by-step walk throughs for math, stats and other disciplines.

Practice Exams
Five different test taking formats for every chapter.

Easy Access
Study any of your books, on any computer, anywhere.

Unlimited Textbooks
All the features above for virtually all your textbooks, just add them to your account at no additional cost.

TRY THE FIRST CHAPTER FREE!

Be sure to use the promo code above when registering on Cram101.com to get 50% off your membership fees.

STUDYING MADE EASY

This CramI0I notebook is designed to make studying easier and increase your comprehension of the textbook material. Instead of starting with a blank notebook and trying to write down everything discussed in class lectures, you can use this CramI0I textbook notebook and annotate your notes along with the lecture.

Our goal is to give you the best tools for success.

For a supreme understanding of the course, pair your notebook with our online tools. Should you decide you prefer CramI0I.com as your study tool,

we'd like to offer you a trade...

Our Trade In program is a simple way for us to keep our promise and provide you the best studying tools, regardless of where you purchased your CramI0I textbook notebook. As long as your notebook is in *Like New Condition**, you can send it back to us and we will immediately give you a CramI0I.com account free for 120 days!

Let The *Trade In* Begin!

THREE SIMPLE STEPS TO TRADE:

1. Go to www.cram101.com/tradein and fill out the packing slip information.

2. Submit and print the packing slip and mail it in with your CramI0I textbook notebook.

3. Activate your account after you receive your email confirmation.

* Books must be returned in *Like New Condition*, meaning there is no damage to the book including, but not limited to; ripped or torn pages, markings or writing on pages, or folded / creased pages. Upon receiving the book, CramI0I will inspect it and reserves the right to terminate your free CramI0I.com account and return your textbook notebook at the owners expense.

Learning System

Cram101 Textbook Outlines is a learning system. The notes in this book are the highlights of your textbook, you will never have to highlight a book again.

How to use this book. Take this book to class, it is your notebook for the lecture. The notes and highlights on the left hand side of the pages follow the outline and order of the textbook. All you have to do is follow along while your instructor presents the lecture. Circle the items emphasized in class and add other important information on the right side. With Cram101 Textbook Outlines you'll spend less time writing and more time listening. Learning becomes more efficient.

Cram101.com Online

Increase your studying efficiency by using Cram101.com's practice tests and online reference material. It is the perfect complement to Cram101 Textbook Outlines. Use self-teaching matching tests or simulate in-class testing with comprehensive multiple choice tests, or simply use Cram's true and false tests for quick review. Cram101.com even allows you to enter your in-class notes for an integrated studying format combining the textbook notes with your class notes.

Visit **www.Cram101.com**, click Sign Up at the top of the screen, and enter **DK73DW12197** in the promo code box on the registration screen. Your access to www.Cram101.com is discounted by 50% because you have purchased this book. Sign up and stop highlighting textbooks forever.

Copyright © 2009 by Cram101, Inc. All rights reserved. "Cram101"® and "Never Highlight a Book Again!"® are registered trademarks of Cram101, Inc. ISBN(s): 9781617441370. PUBI-6.200911

Business Statistics: Contemporary Decision Making
Ken Black, 6th

CONTENTS

1. Introduction to Statistics 2
2. Charts and Graphs 6
3. Descriptive Statistics 16
4. Probability 38
5. Discrete Distributions 48
6. Continuous Distributions 60
7. Sampling and Sampling Distributions 70
8. Statistical Inference: Estimation for Single Populations 86
9. Statistical Inference: Hypothesis Testing for Single Populations 100
10. Statistical Inferences About Two Populations 118
11. Analysis of Variance and Design of Experiments 126
12. Simple Regression Analysis and Correlation 140
13. Multiple Regression Analysis 160
14. Building Multiple Regression Models 168
15. Time-Series Forecasting and Index Numbers 184
16. Analysis of Categorical Data 198
17. Nonparametric Statistics 204
18. Statistical Quality Control 212

Chapter 1. Introduction to Statistics

Sample

In statistics, a Sample is a subset of a population. Typically, the population is very large, making a census or a complete enumeration of all the values in the population impractical or impossible. The Sample represents a subset of manageable size.

Descriptive Statistic

Descriptive statistics are used to describe the main features of a collection of data in quantitative terms. Descriptive statistics are distinguished from inferential statistics (or inductive statistics), in that Descriptive statistics aim to quantitatively summarize a data set, rather than being used to support inferential statements about the population that the data are thought to represent. Even when a data analysis draws its main conclusions using inductive statistical analysis, Descriptive statistics are generally presented along with more formal analyses.

Parameters

In probability theory, one may describe the distribution of a random variable as belonging to a family of probability distributions, distinguished from each other by the values of a finite number of Parameters. For example, one talks about `a Poisson distribution with mean value $\lambda$`. The function defining the distribution (the probability mass function) is:

$$f(k; \lambda) = \frac{e^{-\lambda}\lambda^k}{k!}.$$

This example nicely illustrates the distinction between constants, Parameters, and variables e is Euler`s Number, a fundamental mathematical constant.

Binomial distribution

In probability theory and statistics, the Binomial distribution is the discrete probability distribution of the number of successes in a sequence of n independent yes/no experiments, each of which yields success with probability p. Such a success/failure experiment is also called a Bernoulli experiment or Bernoulli trial. In fact, when n = 1, the Binomial distribution is a Bernoulli distribution.

Ratio data

Ratio data is the continuous data where both differences and ratios are interpretable. Ratio data has a natural zero. The distinctions between interval and ratio data are subtle, but distinction is often not important.

Parametric statistics

Parametric statistics is a branch of statistics that assumes data come from a type of probability distribution and makes inferences about the parameters of the distribution. Most well-known elementary statistical methods are parametric.

Chapter 1. Introduction to Statistics

Chapter 1. Introduction to Statistics

Generally speaking parametric methods make more assumptions than non-parametric methods. If those extra assumptions are correct, parametric methods can produce more accurate and precise estimates. They are said to have more statistical power. However, if those assumptions are incorrect, parametric methods can be very misleading. For that reason they are often not considered robust. On the other hand, parametric formulae are often simpler to write down and faster to compute. In some, but definitely not all cases, their simplicity makes up for their non-robustness, especially if care is taken to examine diagnostic statistics.

Poisson distribution

In probability theory and statistics, the Poisson distribution is a discrete probability distribution that expresses the probability of a number of events occurring in a fixed period of time if these events occur with a known average rate and independently of the time since the last event.

The distribution was first introduced by Siméon-Denis Poisson (1781-1840) and published, together with his probability theory, in 1838 in his work Recherches sur la probabilité des jugements en matière criminelle et en matière civile . The work focused on certain random variables N that count, among other things, the number of discrete occurrences (sometimes called `arrivals`) that take place during a time-interval of given length.

Statistical analysis

Statistical analysis refers to the branch of mathematics that deals with the collection, analysis, interpretation and presentation of masses of numerical data.

ANOVA

In statistics, ANOVA is a collection of statistical models, and their associated procedures, in which the observed variance is partitioned into components due to different sources of variation. In its simplest form ANOVA provides a statistical test of whether or not the means of several groups are all equal, and therefore generalizes Student`s two-sample t-test to more than two groups. ANOVAs are helpful because they possess a certain advantage over a two-sample t-test. Doing multiple two-sample t-tests would result in a largely increased chance of committing a type I error. For this reason, ANOVAs are useful in comparing three or more means.
There are three conceptual classes of such models:

· Fixed-effects models assume that the data came from normal populations which may differ only in their means. (Model 1)

· Random effects models assume that the data describe a hierarchy of different populations whose differences are constrained by the hierarchy. (Model 2)

· Mixed-effect models describe the situations where both fixed and random effects are present. (Model 3)

Chapter 1. Introduction to Statistics

Chapter 2. Charts and Graphs

Grouped data	Grouped data is a statistical term used in data analysis. A raw dataset can be organized by constructing a table showing the frequency distribution of the variable (whose values are given in the raw dataset). Such a frequency table is often referred to as a Grouped data.
Frequency Distribution	In statistics, a Frequency distribution is a tabulation of the values that one or more variables take in a sample.

Univariate Frequency distributions are often presented as lists ordered by quantity showing the number of times each value appears. For example, if 100 people rate a five-point Likert scale assessing their agreement with a statement on a scale on which 1 denotes strong agreement and 5 strong disagreement, the Frequency distribution of their responses might look like:

Rank	Degree of agreement	Number
1	Strongly agree	20
2	Agree somewhat	30
3	Not sure	20
4	Disagree somewhat	15
5	Strongly disagree	15

This simple tabulation has two drawbacks. When a variable can take continuous values instead of discrete values or when the number of possible values is too large, the table becomes less meaningful and more difficult to interpret. A different tabulation scheme aggregates values into bins such that each bin encompasses a range of values.

Range	In descriptive statistics, the Range is the length of the smallest interval which contains all the data. It is calculated by subtracting the smallest observation (sample minimum) from the greatest (sample maximum) and provides an indication of [statistical dispersion] It is measured in the same units as the data. Since it only depends on two of the observations, it is a poor and weak measure of dispersion except when the sample size is large.
Relative frequency	In a series of observations, or trials, the relative frequency of occurrence of an event E is calculated as the number of times the event E happened over the total number of observations made. The relative frequency density of occurrence of an event is the relative frequency of E divided by the size of the bin used to classify E.
Midpoint	The Midpoint is the middle point of a line segment. It is equidistant from both endpoints.

Chapter 2. Charts and Graphs

Chapter 2. Charts and Graphs

The formula for determining the Midpoint of a segment in the plane, with endpoints (x_1) and (x_2) is:

$$\frac{x_1 + x_2}{2}$$

The formula for determining the Midpoint of a segment in the plane, with endpoints (x_1, y_1) and (x_2, y_2) is:

$$\left(\frac{x_1 + x_2}{2}, \frac{y_1 + y_2}{2}\right)$$

The formula for determining the Midpoint of a segment in the plane, with endpoints (x_1, y_1, z_1) and (x_2, y_2 z_2) is:

$$\left(\frac{x_1 + x_2}{2}, \frac{y_1 + y_2}{2}, \frac{z_1 + z_2}{2}\right)$$

More generally, for an n-dimensional space with axes $x_1, x_2, x_3, \ldots, x_n$, the Midpoint of an interval is given by:

$$\left(\frac{x_{1_1} + x_{1_2}}{2}, \frac{x_{2_1} + x_{2_2}}{2}, \frac{x_{3_1} + x_{3_2}}{2}, \ldots, \frac{x_{n_1} + x_{n_2}}{2}\right)$$

.

Histogram

A histogram is a graphical display of tabulated frequencies. That is, a histogram is the graphical version of a table which shows what proportion of cases fall into each of several or many specified categories. The categories are usually specified as nonoverlapping intervals of some variable. The categories bars must be adjacent.

Chapter 2. Charts and Graphs

Chapter 2. Charts and Graphs

Pareto chart	A Pareto chart is a type of chart that contains both bars and a line graph, where individual values are represented in descending order by bars, and the cumulative total is represented by the line. The left vertical axis is the frequency of occurrence, but it can alternatively represent cost or another important unit of measure. The right vertical axis is the cumulative percentage of the total number of occurrences, total cost, or total of the particular unit of measure.
Poisson distribution	In probability theory and statistics, the Poisson distribution is a discrete probability distribution that expresses the probability of a number of events occurring in a fixed period of time if these events occur with a known average rate and independently of the time since the last event. The distribution was first introduced by Siméon-Denis Poisson (1781-1840) and published, together with his probability theory, in 1838 in his work Recherches sur la probabilité des jugements en matière criminelle et en matière civile . The work focused on certain random variables N that count, among other things, the number of discrete occurrences (sometimes called `arrivals`) that take place during a time-interval of given length.
Quantitative data	Quantitative data is data measured or identified on a numerical scale. It can be analysed using statistical methods, and results can be displayed using tables, charts, histograms and graphs.
Bar chart	A Bar chart or bar graph is a chart with rectangular bars with lengths proportional to the values that they represent. The bars can also be plotted horizontally. Bar charts are used for plotting discrete or discontinuous data i.e. data which has discrete values and is not continuous.
Friedman test	The Friedman test is a non-parametric statistical test developed by the U.S. economist Milton Friedman. Similar to the parametric repeated measures ANOVA, it is used to detect differences in treatments across multiple test attempts. The procedure involves ranking each row (or block) together, then considering the values of ranks by columns. Applicable to complete block designs, it is thus a special case of the Durbin test. Classic examples of use are:

Chapter 2. Charts and Graphs

Chapter 2. Charts and Graphs

	· n wine judges rate k different wines. Are any wines ranked consistently higher or lower than the others?
	· n wines are rated by k different judges. Are the judges ratings consistent with each other?
	· n welders use k welding torches, and the ensuing welds were rated on quality. Do any of the torches produce consistently better or worse welds?
Frequency polygon	A frequency polygon is formed by joining the mid-points of the top of the columns of a histogram or the midpoints of the data intervals.
ANOVA	In statistics, ANOVA is a collection of statistical models, and their associated procedures, in which the observed variance is partitioned into components due to different sources of variation. In its simplest form ANOVA provides a statistical test of whether or not the means of several groups are all equal, and therefore generalizes Student`s two-sample t-test to more than two groups. ANOVAs are helpful because they possess a certain advantage over a two-sample t-test. Doing multiple two-sample t-tests would result in a largely increased chance of committing a type I error. For this reason, ANOVAs are useful in comparing three or more means. There are three conceptual classes of such models: · Fixed-effects models assume that the data came from normal populations which may differ only in their means. (Model 1) · Random effects models assume that the data describe a hierarchy of different populations whose differences are constrained by the hierarchy. (Model 2) · Mixed-effect models describe the situations where both fixed and random effects are present. (Model 3)
Ogive	An Ogive is the roundly tapered end of a two-dimensional or three-dimensional object. In statistics, an Ogive is a graph showing the curve of a cumulative distribution function.

Chapter 2. Charts and Graphs

Chapter 2. Charts and Graphs

Qualitative data	The term Qualitative data is used to describe certain types of information. This is almost the converse of quantitative data, in which items are more precisely described data in terms of quantity and in which numerical values are used. However, data originally obtained as qualitative information about individual items may give rise to quantitative data if they are summarised by means of counts.
Six Sigma	Six sigma is a business management strategy, originally developed by Motorola, that today enjoys widespread application in many sectors of industry. six sigma seeks to identify and remove the causes of defects and errors in manufacturing and business processes. It uses a set of quality management methods, including statistical methods, and creates a special infrastructure of people within the organization (`Black Belts` etc.)
Scatter plot	A Scatter plot or scattergraph is a type of mathematical diagram using Cartesian coordinates to display values for two variables for a set of data. The data is displayed as a collection of points, each having the value of one variable determining the position on the horizontal axis and the value of the other variable determining the position on the vertical axis. This kind of plot is also called a scatter chart, scatter diagram and scatter graph.
Numerical Data	Numerical data is data measured or identified on a numerical scale. Numerical data can be analyzed using statistical methods, and results can be displayed using tables, charts, histograms and graphs. For example, a researcher will ask a questions to a participant that include words how often, how many or percentage.

Chapter 2. Charts and Graphs

Chapter 3. Descriptive Statistics

Descriptive statistic	Descriptive statistics are used to describe the main features of a collection of data in quantitative terms. Descriptive statistics are distinguished from inferential statistics (or inductive statistics), in that Descriptive statistics aim to quantitatively summarize a data set, rather than being used to support inferential statements about the population that the data are thought to represent. Even when a data analysis draws its main conclusions using inductive statistical analysis, Descriptive statistics are generally presented along with more formal analyses.
Central tendency	In statistics, the term Central tendency relates to the way in which quantitative data tend to cluster around some value. A measure of Central tendency is any of a number of ways of specifying this `central value`. In practical statistical analyses, the terms are often used before one has chosen even a preliminary form of analysis: thus an initial objective might be to `choose an appropriate measure of Central tendency`.
Grouped data	Grouped data is a statistical term used in data analysis. A raw dataset can be organized by constructing a table showing the frequency distribution of the variable (whose values are given in the raw dataset). Such a frequency table is often referred to as a Grouped data.
Bimodal	In statistics, a Bimodal distribution is a continuous probability distribution with two different modes. These appear as distinct peaks (local maxima) in the probability density function Examples of variables with Bimodal distributions include the time between eruptions of certain geysers, the color of galaxies, the size of worker weaver ants, the age of incidence of Hodgkin`s lymphoma, the speed of inactivation of the drug isoniazid in US adults, and the absolute magnitude of novae. A Bimodal distribution most commonly arises as a mixture of two different unimodal distributions (i.e. distributions having only one mode).
Median	In probability theory and statistics, a median is described as the number separating the higher half of a sample, a population, from the lower half. The median of a finite list of numbers can be found by arranging all the observations from lowest value to highest value and picking the middle one. If there is an even number of observations, the median is not unique, so one often takes the mean of the two middle values.
Mode	In statistics, the Mode is the value that occurs the most frequently in a data set or a probability distribution. In some fields, notably education, sample data are often called scores, and the sample Mode is known as the modal score. Like the statistical mean and the median, the Mode is a way of capturing important information about a random variable or a population in a single quantity.

Chapter 3. Descriptive Statistics

Chapter 3. Descriptive Statistics

ANOVA

In statistics, ANOVA is a collection of statistical models, and their associated procedures, in which the observed variance is partitioned into components due to different sources of variation. In its simplest form ANOVA provides a statistical test of whether or not the means of several groups are all equal, and therefore generalizes Student`s two-sample t-test to more than two groups. ANOVAs are helpful because they possess a certain advantage over a two-sample t-test. Doing multiple two-sample t-tests would result in a largely increased chance of committing a type I error. For this reason, ANOVAs are useful in comparing three or more means.
There are three conceptual classes of such models:

· Fixed-effects models assume that the data came from normal populations which may differ only in their means. (Model 1)

· Random effects models assume that the data describe a hierarchy of different populations whose differences are constrained by the hierarchy. (Model 2)

· Mixed-effect models describe the situations where both fixed and random effects are present. (Model 3)

Mean

In statistics, mean has two related meanings:

· the arithmetic mean .

· the expected value of a random variable, which is also called the population mean.
It is sometimes stated that the `mean` means average. This is incorrect if `mean` is taken in the specific sense of `arithmetic mean` as there are different types of averages: the mean, median, and mode.

Poisson distribution

In probability theory and statistics, the Poisson distribution is a discrete probability distribution that expresses the probability of a number of events occurring in a fixed period of time if these events occur with a known average rate and independently of the time since the last event.

The distribution was first introduced by Siméon-Denis Poisson (1781-1840) and published, together with his probability theory, in 1838 in his work Recherches sur la probabilité des jugements en matière criminelle et en matière civile . The work focused on certain random variables N that count, among other things, the number of discrete occurrences (sometimes called `arrivals`) that take place during a time-interval of given length.

Chapter 3. Descriptive Statistics

Chapter 3. Descriptive Statistics

Quartile	In descriptive statistics, a Quartile is one of four equal groups, representing a fourth of the distributed sampled population. It is a type of quantile. In epidemiology, the four ranges defined by the three values discussed here. · first Quartile = lower Quartile = cuts off lowest 25% of data = 25th percentile · second Quartile = median = cuts data set in half = 50th percentile · third Quartile = upper Quartile = cuts off highest 25% of data, or lowest 75% = 75th percentile The difference between the upper and lower Quartiles is called the interQuartile range.
Mann-Whitney U test	In statistics, the Mann-Whitney U test is a non-parametric test for assessing whether two independent samples of observations come from the same distribution. It is one of the best-known non-parametric significance tests. It was proposed initially by Frank Wilcoxon in 1945, for equal sample sizes, and extended to arbitrary sample sizes and in other ways by H. B. Mann and Whitney (1947).
Range	In descriptive statistics, the Range is the length of the smallest interval which contains all the data. It is calculated by subtracting the smallest observation (sample minimum) from the greatest (sample maximum) and provides an indication of [statistical dispersion] It is measured in the same units as the data. Since it only depends on two of the observations, it is a poor and weak measure of dispersion except when the sample size is large.
Variability	Variability is a measure of how observations in the data set are distributed across various categories. There are many different descriptive statistics that can be chosen as a measurement of the central tendency. In other words, dispersion is quantifiable variation of measurements of differing members of a population within the scale on which they are measured.
Coefficient of variation	In probability theory and statistics, the Coefficient of variation is a normalized measure of dispersion of a probability distribution. It is defined as the ratio of the standard deviation σ to the mean μ :

Chapter 3. Descriptive Statistics

Chapter 3. Descriptive Statistics

$$c_v = \frac{\sigma}{\mu}$$

This is only defined for non-zero mean, and is most useful for variables that are always positive. It is also known as unitized risk or the variation coefficient. It is expressed as percentage.

Interquartile range | In descriptive statistics, the Interquartile range, also called the midspread or middle fifty, is a measure of statistical dispersion, being equal to the difference between the third and first quartiles.

Unlike (total) range, the Interquartile range is a robust statistic, having a breakdown point of 25%, and is thus often preferred to the total range.

The IQR is used to build box plots, simple graphical representations of a probability distribution.

Deviation | In mathematics and statistics, deviation is a measure of difference for interval and ratio variables between the observed value and the mean. The sign of deviation, either positive or negative, indicates whether the observation is larger than or smaller than the mean. The magnitude of the value reports how different (in the relevant numerical scale) an observation is from the mean.

Absolute deviation | In statistics, the Absolute deviation of an element of a data set is the absolute difference between that element and a given point. Typically the point from which the deviation is measured is a measure of central tendency, most often the median or sometimes the mean of the data set.

$$D_i = : x_i - m(X) :$$

where

D_i is the Absolute deviation,
x_i is the data element

Chapter 3. Descriptive Statistics

Chapter 3. Descriptive Statistics

and m(X) is the chosen measure of central tendency of the data set--sometimes the mean , but most often the median.

Population variance

If μ = E(X) is the expected value (mean) of the random variable X, then the population variance is var(X) = E((X - μ)^2).

Sum of squares

Sum of squares is a concept that permeates much of inferential statistics and descriptive statistics. More properly, it is the sum of squared deviations. Mathematically, it is an unscaled, or unadjusted measure of dispersion (also called variability). When scaled for the number of degrees of freedom, it estimates the variance, or spread of the observations about their mean value. The distance from any point in a collection of data, to the mean of the data, is the deviation. This can be written as $X_i - \overline{X}$, where X_i is the ith data point, and $\overline{X}$ is the estimate of the mean. If all such deviations are squared, then summed, as in $\sum_{i=1}^{n} \left(X_i - \overline{X} \right)^2$, we have the `Sum of squares` for these data.

Variance

In probability theory and statistics, the Variance is used as one of several descriptors of a distribution. It describes how far values lie from the mean. In particular, the Variance is one of the moments of a distribution.

Squared Deviations

In probability theory and statistics, the definition of variance is either the expected value (when considering a theoretical distribution), or average value (for actual experimental data), of Squared deviations from the mean. Computations for analysis of variance involve the partitioning of a sum of Squared deviations. An understanding of the complex computations involved is greatly enhanced by a detailed study of the statistical value:

$$E(X^2).$$

It is well-known that for a random variable X with mean μ and variance σ^2:

$$\sigma^2 = E(X^2) - \mu^2$$

Chapter 3. Descriptive Statistics

Chapter 3. Descriptive Statistics

Therefore

$$E(X^2) = \sigma^2 + \mu^2.$$

From the above, the following are easily derived:

$$E\left(\sum (X^2)\right) = n\sigma^2 + n\mu^2$$

$$E\left(\left(\sum X\right)^2\right) = n\sigma^2 + n^2\mu^2$$

The sum of Squared deviations needed to calculate variance (before deciding whether to divide by n or n − 1) is most easily calculated as

$$S = \sum x^2 - \frac{\left(\sum x\right)^2}{n}$$

From the two derived expectations above the expected value of this sum is

$$E(S) = n\sigma^2 + n\mu^2 - \frac{n\sigma^2 + n^2\mu^2}{n}$$

which implies

$$E(S) = (n-1)\sigma^2.$$

Chapter 3. Descriptive Statistics

Chapter 3. Descriptive Statistics

	This effectively proves the use of the divisor n – 1 in the calculation of an unbiased sample estimate of σ².
68-95-99.7 rule	In statistics, the 68-95-99.7 rule or empirical rule, states that for a normal distribution, nearly all values lie within 3 standard deviations of the mean. About 68% of the values lie within 1 standard deviation of the mean. In statistical notation, this is represented as: $\mu \pm \sigma$. About 95% of the values lie within 2 standard deviations of the mean. The statistical notation for this is: $\mu \pm 2\sigma$. Nearly all (99.7%) of the values lie within 3 standard deviations of the mean. Statisticians use the following notation to represent this: $\mu \pm 3\sigma$.
Standard deviation	In probability theory and statistics, the Standard deviation of a statistical population, a data set, or a probability distribution is the square root of its variance. Standard deviation is a widely used measure of the variability or dispersion, being algebraically more tractable though practically less robust than the expected deviation or average absolute deviation. It shows how much variation there is from the `average` (mean, or expected/budgeted value).
Sample	In statistics, a Sample is a subset of a population. Typically, the population is very large, making a census or a complete enumeration of all the values in the population impractical or impossible. The Sample represents a subset of manageable size.
Sample standard deviation	The sample standard deviation measures the variability of data in a sample. It is easy to compute because it is based on a small and manageable sample.
Estimator	In statistics, an Estimator or point estimate is a statistic (that is, a measurable function of the data) that is used to infer the value of an unknown parameter in a statistical model. The parameter being estimated is sometimes called the estimand. It can be either finite-dimensional, or infinite-dimensional (semi-nonparametric and non-parametric models).

Chapter 3. Descriptive Statistics

Chapter 3. Descriptive Statistics

Score

In statistics, the Score or Score function is the partial derivative, with respect to some parameter θ, of the logarithm (commonly the natural logarithm) of the likelihood function. If the observation is X and its likelihood is $L(\theta;X)$, then the Score V can be found through the chain rule:

$$V = \frac{\partial}{\partial \theta} \log L(\theta; X) = \frac{1}{L(\theta; X)} \frac{\partial L(\theta; X)}{\partial \theta}.$$

Note that V is a function of θ and the observation X, so that, in general, it is not a statistic. Note also that V indicates the sensitivity of $L(\theta;X)$ (its variation normalized by its value.)

Statistical dispersion

In statistics, Statistical dispersion is variability or spread in a variable or a probability distribution. Common examples of measures of Statistical dispersion are the variance, standard deviation and interquartile range.

Dispersion is contrasted with location or central tendency, and together they are the most used properties of distributions.

Friedman test

The Friedman test is a non-parametric statistical test developed by the U.S. economist Milton Friedman. Similar to the parametric repeated measures ANOVA, it is used to detect differences in treatments across multiple test attempts. The procedure involves ranking each row (or block) together, then considering the values of ranks by columns. Applicable to complete block designs, it is thus a special case of the Durbin test.

Classic examples of use are:

· n wine judges rate k different wines. Are any wines ranked consistently higher or lower than the others?

· n wines are rated by k different judges. Are the judges ratings consistent with each other?

· n welders use k welding torches, and the ensuing welds were rated on quality. Do any of the torches produce consistently better or worse welds?

Chapter 3. Descriptive Statistics

Chapter 3. Descriptive Statistics

Skewness

In probability theory and statistics, Skewness is a measure of the asymmetry of the probability distribution of a real-valued random variable. The Skewness value can be positive or negative, or even undefined. Qualitatively, a negative skew indicates that the tail on the left side of probability density function is longer than the right side and the bulk of the values (including the median) lie to the right of the mean.

Box plot

In descriptive statistics, a Box plot is a convenient way of graphically depicting groups of numerical data through their five-number summaries: the smallest observation (sample minimum), lower quartile (Q1), median (Q2), upper quartile (Q3), and largest observation (sample maximum). A Box plot may also indicate which observations, if any, might be considered outliers.

Box plots display differences between populations without making any assumptions of the underlying statistical distribution: they are non-parametric. The spacings between the different parts of the box help indicate the degree of dispersion (spread) and skewness in the data, and identify outliers. Box plots can be drawn either horizontally or vertically.

Kurtosis

In probability theory and statistics, Kurtosis is a measure of the `peakedness` of the probability distribution of a real-valued random variable. Higher Kurtosis means more of the variance is the result of infrequent extreme deviations, as opposed to frequent modestly sized deviations.

The fourth standardized moment is defined as

$$\frac{\mu_4}{\sigma^4},$$

where μ_4 is the fourth moment about the mean and σ is the standard deviation.

Leptokurtic

In probability theory and statistics, kurtosis is a measure of the `peakedness` of the probability distribution of a real-valued random variable. Higher kurtosis means more of the variance is due to infrequent extreme deviations, as opposed to frequent modestly sized deviations. The far red light has no effect on the average speed of the gravitropic reaction in wheat coleoptiles, but it changes kurtosis from platykurtic to Leptokurtic
The fourth standardized moment is defined as

Chapter 3. Descriptive Statistics

Chapter 3. Descriptive Statistics

$$\frac{\mu_4}{\sigma^4},$$

where μ_4 is the fourth moment about the mean and σ is the standard deviation.

Platykurtic

In probability theory and statistics, kurtosis is a measure of the `peakedness` of the probability distribution of a real-valued random variable. Higher kurtosis means more of the variance is due to infrequent extreme deviations, as opposed to frequent modestly sized deviations. The far red light has no effect on the average speed of the gravitropic reaction in wheat coleoptiles, but it changes kurtosis from Platykurtic to leptokurtic
The fourth standardized moment is defined as

$$\frac{\mu_4}{\sigma^4},$$

where μ_4 is the fourth moment about the mean and σ is the standard deviation.

Platykurtic distribution

A distribution with negative kurtosis is called platykurtic. In terms of shape, a platykurtic distribution has a smaller "peak" around the mean (that is, a lower probability than a normally distributed variable of values near the mean) and "thin tails" (that is, a lower probability than a normally distributed variable of extreme values).

Sample mean

The Sample mean or empirical mean and the sample covariance are statistics computed from a collection of data.

Given a random sample $\mathbf{x}_1, \ldots, \mathbf{x}_N$ from an n-dimensional random variable $\mathbf{X}$, the Sample mean is

$$\bar{\mathbf{x}} = \frac{1}{N} \sum_{k=1}^{N} \mathbf{x}_k.$$

Chapter 3. Descriptive Statistics

Chapter 3. Descriptive Statistics

In coordinates, writing the vectors as columns,

$$\mathbf{x}_k = \begin{bmatrix} x_{1k} \\ \vdots \\ x_{nk} \end{bmatrix}, \quad \bar{\mathbf{x}} = \begin{bmatrix} \bar{x}_1 \\ \vdots \\ \bar{x}_n \end{bmatrix},$$

the entries of the Sample mean are

$$\bar{x}_i = \frac{1}{N} \sum_{k=1}^{N} x_{ik}, \quad i = 1, \ldots, n.$$

The sample covariance of $\mathbf{x}_1, \ldots, \mathbf{x}_N$ is the n-by-n matrix $\mathbf{Q} = [q_{ij}]$ with the entries given by

$$q_{ij} = \frac{1}{N-1} \sum_{k=1}^{N} (x_{ik} - \bar{x}_i)(x_{jk} - \bar{x}_j)$$

The Sample mean and the sample covariance matrix are unbiased estimates of the mean and the covariance matrix of the random variable $\mathbf{X}$. The reason why the sample covariance matrix has $N - 1$ in the denominator rather than N is essentially that the population mean E(X) is not known and is replaced by the Sample mean $\bar{x}$.

Chapter 3. Descriptive Statistics

Chapter 4. Probability

Range	In descriptive statistics, the Range is the length of the smallest interval which contains all the data. It is calculated by subtracting the smallest observation (sample minimum) from the greatest (sample maximum) and provides an indication of [statistical dispersion] It is measured in the same units as the data. Since it only depends on two of the observations, it is a poor and weak measure of dispersion except when the sample size is large.
Relative frequency	In a series of observations, or trials, the relative frequency of occurrence of an event E is calculated as the number of times the event E happened over the total number of observations made. The relative frequency density of occurrence of an event is the relative frequency of E divided by the size of the bin used to classify E.
Elementary event	In probability theory, an Elementary event or atomic event is a singleton of a sample space. An outcome is an element of a sample space. An Elementary event is a set containing an outcome, not the outcome itself. However, Elementary events are often written as outcomes for simplicity when the difference is unambiguous.
Collectively exhaustive	In probability theory, a set of events is jointly or Collectively exhaustive if at least one of the events must occur. For example, when rolling a six-sided die, the outcomes 1, 2, 3, 4, 5, and 6 are Collectively exhaustive, because they encompass the entire range of possible outcomes. Another way to describe Collectively exhaustive events, is that their union must cover all the events within the entire sample space. For example, events A and B are said to be Collectively exhaustive if $A \cup B = S$ where S is the sample space.
Sample	In statistics, a Sample is a subset of a population. Typically, the population is very large, making a census or a complete enumeration of all the values in the population impractical or impossible. The Sample represents a subset of manageable size.
Sample space	In probability theory, the Sample space or universal Sample space, often denoted S, Ω, or U (for `universe`), of an experiment or random trial is the set of all possible outcomes. For example, if the experiment is tossing a coin, the Sample space is the set {head, tail}. For tossing a single six-sided die, the Sample space is {1, 2, 3, 4, 5, 6}.
Union	In set theory and other branches of mathematics, the union of a collection of sets is the set that contains everything that belongs to any of the sets, but nothing else.

Chapter 4. Probability

Chapter 4. Probability

Complement

In probability theory, the Complement of any event A is the event [not A], i.e. the event that A does not occur. The event A and its Complement [not A] are mutually exclusive and exhaustive. Generally, there is only one event B such that A and B are both mutually exclusive and exhaustive; that event is the Complement of A. The Complement of an event A is usually denoted as A', A^c or $\overline{A}$.

· A coin is flipped and one assumes it cannot land on its edge. It can either land on `heads` or on `tails` Because these two events are Complementary, we have

$$Pr(heads) + Pr(tails) = 1.$$

Correlation

In statistics, Correlation indicates the strength and direction of a relationship between two random variables. The commonest use refers to a linear relationship, but the concept of nonlinear Correlation is also used. In general statistical usage, Correlation or co-relation refers to the departure of two random variables from independence.

Mutually exclusive

In layman`s terms, two events are Mutually exclusive if they cannot occur at the same time (i.e., they have no common outcomes).
In logic, two Mutually exclusive propositions are propositions that logically cannot both be true. Another term f is `disjunct.` To say that more than two propositions are Mutually exclusive may, depending on context mean that no two of them can both be true, or only that they cannot all be true.

ANOVA

In statistics, ANOVA is a collection of statistical models, and their associated procedures, in which the observed variance is partitioned into components due to different sources of variation. In its simplest form ANOVA provides a statistical test of whether or not the means of several groups are all equal, and therefore generalizes Student`s two-sample t-test to more than two groups. ANOVAs are helpful because they possess a certain advantage over a two-sample t-test. Doing multiple two-sample t-tests would result in a largely increased chance of committing a type I error. For this reason, ANOVAs are useful in comparing three or more means.
There are three conceptual classes of such models:

· Fixed-effects models assume that the data came from normal populations which may differ only in their means. (Model 1)

Chapter 4. Probability

Chapter 4. Probability

	· Random effects models assume that the data describe a hierarchy of different populations whose differences are constrained by the hierarchy. (Model 2)
	· Mixed-effect models describe the situations where both fixed and random effects are present. (Model 3)
Statistical inference	Statistical inference is the process of making conclusions using data that is subject to random variation, for example, observational errors or sampling variation. More substantially, the terms Statistical inference, statistical induction and inferential statistics are used to describe systems of procedures that can be used to draw conclusions from datasets arising from systems affected by random variation. Initial requirements of such a system of procedures for inference and induction are that the system should produce reasonable answers when applied to well-defined situations and that it should be general enough to be applied across a range of situations.
Sampling	Sampling is that part of statistical practice concerned with the selection of an unbiased or random subset of individual observations within a population of individuals intended to yield some knowledge about the population of concern, especially for the purposes of making predictions based on statistical inference. Sampling is an important aspect of data collection.
	Researchers rarely survey the entire population for two reasons (Adèr, Mellenbergh, ' Hand, 2008): the cost is too high, and the population is dynamic in that the individuals making up the population may change over time.
Sampling without replacement	Sampling without replacement means that in each successive trial of an experiment or process, the total number of possible outcomes or the mix of possible outcomes is changed by sampling. The probability of future events is thus changed.
Ishikawa diagram	Ishikawa diagrams (also called fishbone diagrams or cause-and-effect diagrams) are diagrams that show the causes of a certain event. Common uses of the Ishikawa diagram are product design and quality defect prevention, to identify potential factors causing an overall effect. Each cause or reason for imperfection is a source of variation.
Rank correlation	In statistics, Rank correlation is the study of relationships between different rankings on the same set of items. A Rank correlation coefficient measures the correspondence between two rankings and assesses its significance.

Chapter 4. Probability

Chapter 4. Probability

Two of the more popular Rank correlation statistics are

· Spearman`s Rank correlation coefficient (Spearman`s ρ)

· Kendall`s tau Rank correlation coefficient (Kendall`s τ)

An increasing Rank correlation coefficient implies increasing agreement between rankings. The coefficient is inside the interval [−1, 1] and assumes the value:

· −1 if the disagreement between the two rankings is perfect; one ranking is the reverse of the other.

· 0 if the rankings are completely independent.

· 1 if the agreement between the two rankings is perfect; the two rankings are the same.

Following the Diaconis reference below, a ranking can be seen as a permutation of a set of objects.

Conditional probability	Conditional probability is the probability of some event A, given the occurrence of some other event B. Conditional probability is written P, and is read `the (conditional) probability of A, given B` or `the probability of A under the condition B`. When in a random experiment the event B is known to have occurred, the possible outcomes of the experiment are reduced to B, and hence the probability of the occurrence of A is changed from the unConditional probability into the Conditional probability given B.
	Joint probability is the probability of two events in conjunction. That is, it is the probability of both events together. The joint probability of A and B is written $P(A \cap B), P(AB)$ or $P(A,B)$
Probability sampling	Probability sampling is technique of sampling that uses som form of random selection. In order to have randon selection, there must be a set up process that assuraes that the different units in the population have equal probabilities of being chosen.

Chapter 4. Probability

Chapter 4. Probability

Mann-Whitney U test	In statistics, the Mann-Whitney U test is a non-parametric test for assessing whether two independent samples of observations come from the same distribution. It is one of the best-known non-parametric significance tests. It was proposed initially by Frank Wilcoxon in 1945, for equal sample sizes, and extended to arbitrary sample sizes and in other ways by H. B. Mann and Whitney (1947).
Tree diagram	In mathematics and statistical methods, a Tree diagram is used to determine the probability of getting specific results where the possibilities are nested.

Chapter 4. Probability

Chapter 5. Discrete Distributions

Continuous	In probability theory, a probability distribution is called continuous if its cumulative distribution function is continuous. This is equivalent to saying that for random variables X with the distribution in question, $Pr[X = a] = 0$ for all real numbers a, i.e.: the probability that X attains the value a is zero, for any number a. If the distribution of X is continuous then X is called a continuous random variable.
Continuous random variable	In probability theory, a probability distribution is called continuous if its cumulative distribution function is continuous. This is equivalent to saying that for random variables X with the distribution in question, $Pr[X = a] = 0$ for all real numbers a, i.e.: the probability that X attains the value a is zero, for any number a. If the distribution of X is continuous then X is called a Continuous random variable.
Random variable	In mathematics, a Random variable is (in general) a measurable function that maps a probability space into a measurable space. Random variables mapping all possible outcomes of an event into the real numbers are frequently studied in elementary statistics and used in the sciences to make predictions based on data obtained from scientific experiments. In addition to scientific applications, Random variables were developed for the analysis of games of chance and stochastic events.
ANOVA	In statistics, ANOVA is a collection of statistical models, and their associated procedures, in which the observed variance is partitioned into components due to different sources of variation. In its simplest form ANOVA provides a statistical test of whether or not the means of several groups are all equal, and therefore generalizes Student's two-sample t-test to more than two groups. ANOVAs are helpful because they possess a certain advantage over a two-sample t-test. Doing multiple two-sample t-tests would result in a largely increased chance of committing a type I error. For this reason, ANOVAs are useful in comparing three or more means. There are three conceptual classes of such models: · Fixed-effects models assume that the data came from normal populations which may differ only in their means. (Model 1) · Random effects models assume that the data describe a hierarchy of different populations whose differences are constrained by the hierarchy. (Model 2) · Mixed-effect models describe the situations where both fixed and random effects are present. (Model 3)

Chapter 5. Discrete Distributions

Chapter 5. Discrete Distributions

Expected value	In probability theory and statistics, the Expected value of a random variable is the integral of the random variable with respect to its probability measure.
	For discrete random variables this is equivalent to the probability-weighted sum of the possible values.
	For continuous random variables with a density function it is the probability density-weighted integral of the possible values.
Mean	In statistics, mean has two related meanings:
	· the arithmetic mean .
	· the expected value of a random variable, which is also called the population mean. It is sometimes stated that the `mean` means average. This is incorrect if `mean` is taken in the specific sense of `arithmetic mean` as there are different types of averages: the mean, median, and mode.
Binomial distribution	In probability theory and statistics, the Binomial distribution is the discrete probability distribution of the number of successes in a sequence of n independent yes/no experiments, each of which yields success with probability p. Such a success/failure experiment is also called a Bernoulli experiment or Bernoulli trial. In fact, when n = 1, the Binomial distribution is a Bernoulli distribution.
Deviation	In mathematics and statistics, deviation is a measure of difference for interval and ratio variables between the observed value and the mean. The sign of deviation, either positive or negative, indicates whether the observation is larger than or smaller than the mean. The magnitude of the value reports how different (in the relevant numerical scale) an observation is from the mean.
Standard deviation	In probability theory and statistics, the Standard deviation of a statistical population, a data set, or a probability distribution is the square root of its variance. Standard deviation is a widely used measure of the variability or dispersion, being algebraically more tractable though practically less robust than the expected deviation or average absolute deviation.
	It shows how much variation there is from the `average` (mean, or expected/budgeted value).

Chapter 5. Discrete Distributions

Chapter 5. Discrete Distributions

Variance	In probability theory and statistics, the Variance is used as one of several descriptors of a distribution. It describes how far values lie from the mean. In particular, the Variance is one of the moments of a distribution.
Normal distribution	In probability theory and statistics, the Normal distribution or Gaussian distribution is a continuous probability distribution that describes data that cluster around a mean or average. The graph of the associated probability density function is bell-shaped, with a peak at the mean, and is known as the Gaussian function or bell curve. The Gaussian distribution is one of many things named after Carl Friedrich Gauss, who used it to analyze astronomical data, and determined the formula for its probability density function.
Sequence	In mathematics, a sequence is an ordered list of objects (or events). Like a set, it contains members (also called elements or terms), and the number of terms (possibly infinite) is called the length of the sequence. Unlike a set, order matters, and the exact same elements can appear multiple times at different positions in the sequence.
Parameters	In probability theory, one may describe the distribution of a random variable as belonging to a family of probability distributions, distinguished from each other by the values of a finite number of Parameters. For example, one talks about `a Poisson distribution with mean value $\lambda$`. The function defining the distribution (the probability mass function) is: $$f(k;\lambda) = \frac{e^{-\lambda}\lambda^k}{k!}.$$ This example nicely illustrates the distinction between constants, Parameters, and variables e is Euler`s Number, a fundamental mathematical constant.
Variability	Variability is a measure of how observations in the data set are distributed across various categories. There are many different descriptive statistics that can be chosen as a measurement of the central tendency. In other words, dispersion is quantifiable variation of measurements of differing members of a population within the scale on which they are measured.
Poisson distribution	In probability theory and statistics, the Poisson distribution is a discrete probability distribution that expresses the probability of a number of events occurring in a fixed period of time if these events occur with a known average rate and independently of the time since the last event.

Chapter 5. Discrete Distributions

Chapter 5. Discrete Distributions

The distribution was first introduced by Siméon-Denis Poisson (1781-1840) and published, together with his probability theory, in 1838 in his work Recherches sur la probabilité des jugements en matière criminelle et en matière civile . The work focused on certain random variables N that count, among other things, the number of discrete occurrences (sometimes called `arrivals`) that take place during a time-interval of given length.

Collectively exhaustive

In probability theory, a set of events is jointly or Collectively exhaustive if at least one of the events must occur. For example, when rolling a six-sided die, the outcomes 1, 2, 3, 4, 5, and 6 are Collectively exhaustive, because they encompass the entire range of possible outcomes.

Another way to describe Collectively exhaustive events, is that their union must cover all the events within the entire sample space. For example, events A and B are said to be Collectively exhaustive if $A \cup B = S$ where S is the sample space.

Hypergeometric distribution

In probability theory and statistics, the hypergeometric distribution is a discrete probability distribution that describes the number of successes in a sequence of n draws from a finite population without replacement, just as the binomial distribution describes the number of successes for draws with replacement.
The notation is illustrated by this contingency table:

Here N represents the size of the population, m represents the number of successes in the population, k represents the number of successful draws observed, and n represents the number of draws.

A random variable X follows the hypergeometric distribution with parameters N, m and n if the probability is given by

$$P(X = k) = \frac{\binom{m}{k}\binom{N-m}{n-k}}{\binom{N}{n}}.$$

where the binomial coefficient $\binom{a}{b}$ is defined to be the coefficient of x^b in the polynomial expansion of $(1 + x)^a$

Chapter 5. Discrete Distributions

Chapter 5. Discrete Distributions

The probability is positive when k is between max(0, n + m − N) and min(m, n).

Friedman test

The Friedman test is a non-parametric statistical test developed by the U.S. economist Milton Friedman. Similar to the parametric repeated measures ANOVA, it is used to detect differences in treatments across multiple test attempts. The procedure involves ranking each row (or block) together, then considering the values of ranks by columns. Applicable to complete block designs, it is thus a special case of the Durbin test.

Classic examples of use are:

· n wine judges rate k different wines. Are any wines ranked consistently higher or lower than the others?

· n wines are rated by k different judges. Are the judges ratings consistent with each other?

· n welders use k welding torches, and the ensuing welds were rated on quality. Do any of the torches produce consistently better or worse welds?

Binomial probability

Binomial probability typically deals with the probability of several successive decisions, each of which has two possible outcomes.

The probability of an event can be expressed as a Binomial probability if its outcomes can be broken down into two probabilities p and q, where p and q are complementary For example, tossing a coin can be either heads or tails, each which have a (theoretical) probability of 0.5. Rolling a four on a six-sided die can be expressed as the probability (1/6) of getting a 4 or the probability (5/6) of rolling something else.

If an event has a probability, p, of happening, then the probability of it happening twice is p^2, and in general p^n for n successive trials. If we want to know the probability of rolling a die three times and getting two fours and one other number (in that specific order) it becomes:

Chapter 5. Discrete Distributions

Chapter 5. Discrete Distributions

$$\begin{aligned}
P(\text{2 rolls of four and 1 other}) &= P(\text{2 rolls of four})P(\text{1 other}) \\
&= P(\text{rolls of four})^2 P(\text{other})^1 \\
&= (\tfrac{1}{6})^2(\tfrac{5}{6})^1 \\
&= 2.3\%
\end{aligned}$$

Chapter 5. Discrete Distributions

Chapter 6. Continuous Distributions

Continuous

In probability theory, a probability distribution is called continuous if its cumulative distribution function is continuous. This is equivalent to saying that for random variables X with the distribution in question, Pr[X = a] = 0 for all real numbers a, i.e.: the probability that X attains the value a is zero, for any number a. If the distribution of X is continuous then X is called a continuous random variable.

Probability density function

In probability theory, a Probability density function of a continuous random variable is a function that describes the relative likelihood for this random variable to occur at a given point in the observation space. The probability of a random variable falling within a given set is given by the integral of its density over the set.

A Probability density function is most commonly associated with continuous univariate distributions. A random variable X has density f, where f is a non-negative Lebesgue-integrable function, if:

$$P[a \leq X \leq b] = \int_a^b f(x)\,dx.$$

Hence, if F is the cumulative distribution function of X, then:

$$F(x) = \int_{-\infty}^x f(u)\,du,$$

and (if f is continuous at x)

$$f(x) = \frac{d}{dx}F(x).$$

Intuitively, one can think of f(x) dx as being the probability of X falling within the infinitesimal interval [x, x + dx].

Uniform distribution

In mathematics, the uniform distributions are simple probability distributions. There are two types: the discrete uniform distribution; the continuous uniform distribution.

Chapter 6. Continuous Distributions

Chapter 6. Continuous Distributions

Exponential distribution	In probability theory and statistics, the Exponential distributions (a.k.a. negative Exponential distributions) are a class of continuous probability distributions. They describe the times between events in a Poisson process, i.e. a process in which events occur continuously and independently at a constant average rate.

The probability density function (pdf) of an Exponential distribution is

$$f(x; \lambda) = \begin{cases} \lambda e^{-\lambda x}, & x \geq 0, \\ 0, & x < 0. \end{cases}$$

Here $\lambda > 0$ is the parameter of the distribution, often called the rate parameter. The distribution is supported on the interval $[0, \infty)$. If a random variable X has this distribution, we write $X \sim Exp(\lambda)$.

Poisson distribution	In probability theory and statistics, the Poisson distribution is a discrete probability distribution that expresses the probability of a number of events occurring in a fixed period of time if these events occur with a known average rate and independently of the time since the last event.

The distribution was first introduced by Siméon-Denis Poisson (1781-1840) and published, together with his probability theory, in 1838 in his work Recherches sur la probabilité des jugements en matière criminelle et en matière civile . The work focused on certain random variables N that count, among other things, the number of discrete occurrences (sometimes called `arrivals`) that take place during a time-interval of given length.

Deviation	In mathematics and statistics, deviation is a measure of difference for interval and ratio variables between the observed value and the mean. The sign of deviation, either positive or negative, indicates whether the observation is larger than or smaller than the mean. The magnitude of the value reports how different (in the relevant numerical scale) an observation is from the mean.
Mean	In statistics, mean has two related meanings:

· the arithmetic mean .

· the expected value of a random variable, which is also called the population mean.

Chapter 6. Continuous Distributions

Chapter 6. Continuous Distributions

	It is sometimes stated that the `mean` means average. This is incorrect if `mean` is taken in the specific sense of `arithmetic mean` as there are different types of averages: the mean, median, and mode.
Standard deviation	In probability theory and statistics, the Standard deviation of a statistical population, a data set, or a probability distribution is the square root of its variance. Standard deviation is a widely used measure of the variability or dispersion, being algebraically more tractable though practically less robust than the expected deviation or average absolute deviation. It shows how much variation there is from the `average` (mean, or expected/budgeted value).
ANOVA	In statistics, ANOVA is a collection of statistical models, and their associated procedures, in which the observed variance is partitioned into components due to different sources of variation. In its simplest form ANOVA provides a statistical test of whether or not the means of several groups are all equal, and therefore generalizes Student`s two-sample t-test to more than two groups. ANOVAs are helpful because they possess a certain advantage over a two-sample t-test. Doing multiple two-sample t-tests would result in a largely increased chance of committing a type I error. For this reason, ANOVAs are useful in comparing three or more means. There are three conceptual classes of such models: · Fixed-effects models assume that the data came from normal populations which may differ only in their means. (Model 1) · Random effects models assume that the data describe a hierarchy of different populations whose differences are constrained by the hierarchy. (Model 2) · Mixed-effect models describe the situations where both fixed and random effects are present. (Model 3)
Normal distribution	In probability theory and statistics, the Normal distribution or Gaussian distribution is a continuous probability distribution that describes data that cluster around a mean or average. The graph of the associated probability density function is bell-shaped, with a peak at the mean, and is known as the Gaussian function or bell curve. The Gaussian distribution is one of many things named after Carl Friedrich Gauss, who used it to analyze astronomical data, and determined the formula for its probability density function.

Chapter 6. Continuous Distributions

Chapter 6. Continuous Distributions

Type II error	In statistics, the terms type I error (also, α error, false alarm rate (FAR) or false positive) and Type II error (β error) are used to describe possible errors made in a statistical decision process. In 1928, Jerzy Neyman (1894-1981) and Egon Pearson (1895-1980), both eminent statisticians, discussed the problems associated with `deciding whether or not a particular sample may be judged as likely to have been randomly drawn from a certain population` (1928/1967, p.1): and identified `two sources of error`, namely: Type I (α): reject the null hypothesis when the null hypothesis is true, and Type II (β): fail to reject the null hypothesis when the null hypothesis is false In 1930, they elaborated on these two sources of error, remarking that `in testing hypotheses two considerations must be kept in view, (1) we must be able to reduce the chance of rejecting a true hypothesis to as low a value as desired; (2) the test must be so devised that it will reject the hypothesis tested when it is likely to be false.` Scientists recognize two different sorts of error: · Statistical error: the difference between a computed, estimated, or measured value and the true, specified, or theoretically correct value that is caused by random, and inherently unpredictable fluctuations in the measurement apparatus or the system being studied. · Systematic error: the difference between a computed, estimated, or measured value and the true, specified, or theoretically correct value that is caused by non-random fluctuations from an unknown source , and which, once identified, can usually be eliminated. Statisticians speak of two significant sorts of statistical error. The context is that there is a `null hypothesis` which corresponds to a presumed default `state of nature`, e.g., that an individual is free of disease, that an accused is innocent, or that a potential login candidate is not authorized.
Binomial distribution	In probability theory and statistics, the Binomial distribution is the discrete probability distribution of the number of successes in a sequence of n independent yes/no experiments, each of which yields success with probability p. Such a success/failure experiment is also called a Bernoulli experiment or Bernoulli trial. In fact, when n = 1, the Binomial distribution is a Bernoulli distribution.

Chapter 6. Continuous Distributions

Chapter 6. Continuous Distributions

Mann-Whitney U test	In statistics, the Mann-Whitney U test is a non-parametric test for assessing whether two independent samples of observations come from the same distribution. It is one of the best-known non-parametric significance tests. It was proposed initially by Frank Wilcoxon in 1945, for equal sample sizes, and extended to arbitrary sample sizes and in other ways by H. B. Mann and Whitney (1947).
Parameters	In probability theory, one may describe the distribution of a random variable as belonging to a family of probability distributions, distinguished from each other by the values of a finite number of Parameters. For example, one talks about `a Poisson distribution with mean value $\lambda$`. The function defining the distribution (the probability mass function) is: $$f(k; \lambda) = \frac{e^{-\lambda}\lambda^k}{k!}.$$ This example nicely illustrates the distinction between constants, Parameters, and variables e is Euler`s Number, a fundamental mathematical constant.
Exponential function	In mathematics, the exponential function is the function e^x, where e is the number (approximately 2.718) such that the function e^x equals its own derivative. The exponential function is used to model phenomena when a constant change in the independent variable gives the same proportional change (increase or decrease) in the dependent variable. The exponential function is also often written as exp(x), especially when x is an expression complicated enough to make typesetting it as an exponent unwieldy.

Chapter 6. Continuous Distributions

Chapter 7. Sampling and Sampling Distributions

Sampling	Sampling is that part of statistical practice concerned with the selection of an unbiased or random subset of individual observations within a population of individuals intended to yield some knowledge about the population of concern, especially for the purposes of making predictions based on statistical inference. Sampling is an important aspect of data collection. Researchers rarely survey the entire population for two reasons (Adèr, Mellenbergh, ' Hand, 2008): the cost is too high, and the population is dynamic in that the individuals making up the population may change over time.
Random sampling	In random sampling every combination of items from the frame, or stratum, has a known probability of occurring, but these probabilities are not necessarily equal. With any form of sampling there is a risk that the sample may not adequately represent the population but with random sampling there is a large body of statistical theory which quantifies the risk and thus enables an appropriate sample size to be chosen.
Nonprobability sampling	Sampling is the use of a subset of the population to represent the whole population. Probability sampling, or random sampling, is a sampling technique in which the probability of getting any particular sample may be calculated. Nonprobability sampling does not meet this criterion and should be used with caution. Nonprobability sampling techniques cannot be used to infer from the sample to the general population. Any generalizations obtained from a nonprobability sample must be filtered through one`s knowledge of the topic being studied. Performing Nonprobability sampling is considerably less expensive than doing probability sampling, but the results are of limited value.
Simple random sample	A a simple random sample is a group of subjects chosen from a larger group. Each subject from the population is chosen randomly and entirely by chance, such that each subject has the same probability of being chosen at any stage during the sampling process. This process and technique is known as Simple Random Sampling.
Sampling Frame	Sampling frame must be representative of the population and this is a question outside the scope of statistical theory demanding the judgment of experts in the particular subject matter being studied. There is however, a strong division of views about the acceptability of representative sampling across different domains of study. To the philosopher, representative sampling procedure has no justification whatsoever because it is not how truth is pursued in philosophy.
Systematic sample	A systematic sample is a statistical method involving the selection of a specific interval element from a sampling frame. Using this procedure each element in the population has a known and equal probability of selection. This makes it functionally similar to simple random sampling.

Chapter 7. Sampling and Sampling Distributions

Chapter 7. Sampling and Sampling Distributions

Cluster sampling	Cluster sampling is a sampling technique used when `natural` groupings are evident in a statistical population. It is often used in marketing research. In this technique, the total population is divided into these groups (or clusters) and a sample of the groups is selected.
Accidental sampling	Accidental sampling is a type of nonprobability sampling which involves the sample being drawn from that part of the population which is close to hand. That is, a sample population selected because it is readily available and convenient. The researcher using such a sample cannot scientifically make generalizations about the total population from this sample because it would not be representative enough.
Quota sampling	In Quota sampling, the population is first segmented into mutually exclusive sub-groups, just as in stratified sampling. Then judgment is used to select the subjects or units from each segment based on a specified proportion. For example, an interviewer may be told to sample 200 females and 300 males between the age of 45 and 60.
	It is this second step which makes the technique one of non-probability sampling. In Quota sampling, the selection of the sample is non-random unlike random sampling and can often be found unreliable. For example interviewers might be tempted to interview those people in the street who look most helpful, or may choose to use accidental sampling to question those which are closest to them, for time-keeping sake. The problem is that these samples may be biased because not everyone gets a chance of selection. This non-random element is its greatest weakness and quota versus probability has been a matter of controversy for many years.
68-95-99.7 rule	In statistics, the 68-95-99.7 rule or empirical rule, states that for a normal distribution, nearly all values lie within 3 standard deviations of the mean.
	About 68% of the values lie within 1 standard deviation of the mean . In statistical notation, this is represented as: $\mu \pm \sigma$.
	About 95% of the values lie within 2 standard deviations of the mean . The statistical notation for this is: $\mu \pm 2\sigma$.
	Nearly all (99.7%) of the values lie within 3 standard deviations of the mean . Statisticians use the following notation to represent this: $\mu \pm 3\sigma$.

Chapter 7. Sampling and Sampling Distributions

Chapter 7. Sampling and Sampling Distributions

Sampling error	In statistics, Sampling error or estimation error is the error caused by observing a sample instead of the whole population. The Sampling error can be found by subtracting the value of a parameter from the value of a statistic. An estimate of a quantity of interest, such as an average or percentage, will generally be subject to sample-to-sample variation.
Snowball sampling	In sociology and statistics research, Snowball sampling is a technique for developing a research sample where existing study subjects recruit future subjects from among their acquaintances. Thus the sample group appears to grow like a rolling snowball. As the sample builds up, enough data is gathered to be useful for research.
Standard deviation	In probability theory and statistics, the Standard deviation of a statistical population, a data set, or a probability distribution is the square root of its variance. Standard deviation is a widely used measure of the variability or dispersion, being algebraically more tractable though practically less robust than the expected deviation or average absolute deviation. It shows how much variation there is from the `average` (mean, or expected/budgeted value).
Poisson distribution	In probability theory and statistics, the Poisson distribution is a discrete probability distribution that expresses the probability of a number of events occurring in a fixed period of time if these events occur with a known average rate and independently of the time since the last event. The distribution was first introduced by Siméon-Denis Poisson (1781-1840) and published, together with his probability theory, in 1838 in his work Recherches sur la probabilité des jugements en matière criminelle et en matière civile . The work focused on certain random variables N that count, among other things, the number of discrete occurrences (sometimes called `arrivals`) that take place during a time-interval of given length.
Sample	In statistics, a Sample is a subset of a population. Typically, the population is very large, making a census or a complete enumeration of all the values in the population impractical or impossible. The Sample represents a subset of manageable size.
Sample mean	The Sample mean or empirical mean and the sample covariance are statistics computed from a collection of data.

Chapter 7. Sampling and Sampling Distributions

Chapter 7. Sampling and Sampling Distributions

Given a random sample $\mathbf{x}_1, \ldots, \mathbf{x}_N$ from an n-dimensional random variable $\mathbf{X}$, the Sample mean is

$$\bar{\mathbf{x}} = \frac{1}{N} \sum_{k=1}^{N} \mathbf{x}_k.$$

In coordinates, writing the vectors as columns,

$$\mathbf{x}_k = \begin{bmatrix} x_{1k} \\ \vdots \\ x_{nk} \end{bmatrix}, \quad \bar{\mathbf{x}} = \begin{bmatrix} \bar{x}_1 \\ \vdots \\ \bar{x}_n \end{bmatrix},$$

the entries of the Sample mean are

$$\bar{x}_i = \frac{1}{N} \sum_{k=1}^{N} x_{ik}, \quad i = 1, \ldots, n.$$

The sample covariance of $\mathbf{x}_1, \ldots, \mathbf{x}_N$ is the n-by-n matrix $\mathbf{Q} = [q_{ij}]$ with the entries given by

$$q_{ij} = \frac{1}{N-1} \sum_{k=1}^{N} (x_{ik} - \bar{x}_i)(x_{jk} - \bar{x}_j)$$

Chapter 7. Sampling and Sampling Distributions

Chapter 7. Sampling and Sampling Distributions

The Sample mean and the sample covariance matrix are unbiased estimates of the mean and the covariance matrix of the random variable X. The reason why the sample covariance matrix has $N - 1$ in the denominator rather than N is essentially that the population mean E(X) is not known and is replaced by the Sample mean $\bar{x}$.

Sampling distribution	In statistics, a Sampling distribution or finite-sample distribution is the distribution of a given statistic based on a random sample of size n. It may be considered as the distribution of the statistic for all possible samples of a given size. The Sampling distribution depends on the underlying distribution of the population, the statistic being considered, and the sample size used. The Sampling distribution is frequently opposed to the asymptotic distribution, which corresponds to the limit case n → ∞.
Central limit theorem	In probability theory, the Central limit theorem states conditions under which the mean of a sufficiently large number of independent random variables, each with finite mean and variance, will be approximately normally distributed (Rice 1995). The Central limit theorem also requires the random variables to be identically distributed, unless certain conditions are met. Since real-world quantities are often the balanced sum of many unobserved random events, this theorem provides a partial explanation for the prevalence of the normal probability distribution.
Uniform distribution	In mathematics, the uniform distributions are simple probability distributions. There are two types: the discrete uniform distribution; the continuous uniform distribution.
Histogram	A histogram is a graphical display of tabulated frequencies. That is, a histogram is the graphical version of a table which shows what proportion of cases fall into each of several or many specified categories. The categories are usually specified as nonoverlapping intervals of some variable. The categories bars must be adjacent.
Sample size	The sample size of a statistical sample is the number of repeated measurements that constitute it. It is typically denoted n, and is a non-negative integer natural number.
Normal distribution	In probability theory and statistics, the Normal distribution or Gaussian distribution is a continuous probability distribution that describes data that cluster around a mean or average. The graph of the associated probability density function is bell-shaped, with a peak at the mean, and is known as the Gaussian function or bell curve. The Gaussian distribution is one of many things named after Carl Friedrich Gauss, who used it to analyze astronomical data, and determined the formula for its probability density function.

Chapter 7. Sampling and Sampling Distributions

Chapter 7. Sampling and Sampling Distributions

Standard error	The Standard error of a method of measurement or estimation is the standard deviation of the sampling distribution associated with the estimation method. The term may also be used to refer to an estimate of that standard deviation, derived from a particular sample used to compute the estimate. For example, the sample mean is the usual estimator of a population mean. However, different samples drawn from that same population would in general have different values of the sample mean. The Standard error of the mean is the standard deviation of those sample means over all possible samples (of a given size) drawn from the population. Secondly, the Standard error of the mean can refer to an estimate of that standard deviation, computed from the sample of data being analysed at the time.
Sample proportion	Sample proportion is the fraction of samples which were successes. The proportion of successes in the sample is also a random variable.
ANOVA	In statistics, ANOVA is a collection of statistical models, and their associated procedures, in which the observed variance is partitioned into components due to different sources of variation. In its simplest form ANOVA provides a statistical test of whether or not the means of several groups are all equal, and therefore generalizes Student`s two-sample t-test to more than two groups. ANOVAs are helpful because they possess a certain advantage over a two-sample t-test. Doing multiple two-sample t-tests would result in a largely increased chance of committing a type I error. For this reason, ANOVAs are useful in comparing three or more means. There are three conceptual classes of such models: · Fixed-effects models assume that the data came from normal populations which may differ only in their means. (Model 1) · Random effects models assume that the data describe a hierarchy of different populations whose differences are constrained by the hierarchy. (Model 2) · Mixed-effect models describe the situations where both fixed and random effects are present. (Model 3)
Confidence interval	In statistics, a Confidence interval is a particular kind of interval estimate of a population parameter. Instead of estimating the parameter by a single value, an interval likely to include the parameter is given. Thus, Confidence intervals are used to indicate the reliability of an estimate.

Chapter 7. Sampling and Sampling Distributions

Chapter 7. Sampling and Sampling Distributions

Parameters

In probability theory, one may describe the distribution of a random variable as belonging to a family of probability distributions, distinguished from each other by the values of a finite number of Parameters. For example, one talks about `a Poisson distribution with mean value λ`. The function defining the distribution (the probability mass function) is:

$$f(k; \lambda) = \frac{e^{-\lambda}\lambda^k}{k!}.$$

This example nicely illustrates the distinction between constants, Parameters, and variables e is Euler`s Number, a fundamental mathematical constant.

Binomial distribution

In probability theory and statistics, the Binomial distribution is the discrete probability distribution of the number of successes in a sequence of n independent yes/no experiments, each of which yields success with probability p. Such a success/failure experiment is also called a Bernoulli experiment or Bernoulli trial. In fact, when n = 1, the Binomial distribution is a Bernoulli distribution.

Interval estimation

In statistics, Interval estimation is the use of sample data to calculate an interval of possible values of an unknown population parameter, in contrast to point estimation, which is a single number. Neyman (1937) identified Interval estimation as distinct from point estimation (`estimation by unique estimate`). In doing so, he recognised that then-recent work quoting results in the form of an estimate plus-or-minus a standard deviation indicated that Interval estimation was actually the problem statisticians really had in mind.

The most prevalent forms of Interval estimation are:

· confidence intervals (a frequentist method); and

· credible intervals (a Bayesian method).

Other common approaches to Interval estimation, which are encompassed by statistical theory, are:

· Tolerance intervals

Chapter 7. Sampling and Sampling Distributions

Chapter 7. Sampling and Sampling Distributions

· Prediction intervals - used mainly in Regression Analysis

There is a third approach to statistical inference, namely fiducial inference, that also considers Interval estimation.

Estimator

In statistics, an Estimator or point estimate is a statistic (that is, a measurable function of the data) that is used to infer the value of an unknown parameter in a statistical model. The parameter being estimated is sometimes called the estimand. It can be either finite-dimensional, or infinite-dimensional (semi-nonparametric and non-parametric models).

Chapter 7. Sampling and Sampling Distributions

Chapter 8. Statistical Inference: Estimation for Single Populations

Statistical inference — Statistical inference is the process of making conclusions using data that is subject to random variation, for example, observational errors or sampling variation. More substantially, the terms Statistical inference, statistical induction and inferential statistics are used to describe systems of procedures that can be used to draw conclusions from datasets arising from systems affected by random variation. Initial requirements of such a system of procedures for inference and induction are that the system should produce reasonable answers when applied to well-defined situations and that it should be general enough to be applied across a range of situations.

Parameters — In probability theory, one may describe the distribution of a random variable as belonging to a family of probability distributions, distinguished from each other by the values of a finite number of Parameters. For example, one talks about `a Poisson distribution with mean value $\lambda$`. The function defining the distribution (the probability mass function) is:

$$f(k; \lambda) = \frac{e^{-\lambda} \lambda^k}{k!}.$$

This example nicely illustrates the distinction between constants, Parameters, and variables e is Euler`s Number, a fundamental mathematical constant.

Binomial distribution — In probability theory and statistics, the Binomial distribution is the discrete probability distribution of the number of successes in a sequence of n independent yes/no experiments, each of which yields success with probability p. Such a success/failure experiment is also called a Bernoulli experiment or Bernoulli trial. In fact, when n = 1, the Binomial distribution is a Bernoulli distribution.

Sample — In statistics, a Sample is a subset of a population. Typically, the population is very large, making a census or a complete enumeration of all the values in the population impractical or impossible. The Sample represents a subset of manageable size.

Tree diagram — In mathematics and statistical methods, a Tree diagram is used to determine the probability of getting specific results where the possibilities are nested.

Mann-Whitney U test — In statistics, the Mann-Whitney U test is a non-parametric test for assessing whether two independent samples of observations come from the same distribution. It is one of the best-known non-parametric significance tests. It was proposed initially by Frank Wilcoxon in 1945, for equal sample sizes, and extended to arbitrary sample sizes and in other ways by H. B. Mann and Whitney (1947).

Chapter 8. Statistical Inference: Estimation for Single Populations

Chapter 8. Statistical Inference: Estimation for Single Populations

Estimator

In statistics, an Estimator or point estimate is a statistic (that is, a measurable function of the data) that is used to infer the value of an unknown parameter in a statistical model. The parameter being estimated is sometimes called the estimand. It can be either finite-dimensional , or infinite-dimensional (semi-nonparametric and non-parametric models).

Poisson distribution

In probability theory and statistics, the Poisson distribution is a discrete probability distribution that expresses the probability of a number of events occurring in a fixed period of time if these events occur with a known average rate and independently of the time since the last event.

The distribution was first introduced by Siméon-Denis Poisson (1781-1840) and published, together with his probability theory, in 1838 in his work Recherches sur la probabilité des jugements en matière criminelle et en matière civile . The work focused on certain random variables N that count, among other things, the number of discrete occurrences (sometimes called `arrivals`) that take place during a time-interval of given length.

Mean

In statistics, mean has two related meanings:

· the arithmetic mean .

· the expected value of a random variable, which is also called the population mean.
It is sometimes stated that the `mean` means average. This is incorrect if `mean` is taken in the specific sense of `arithmetic mean` as there are different types of averages: the mean, median, and mode.

Confidence interval

In statistics, a Confidence interval is a particular kind of interval estimate of a population parameter. Instead of estimating the parameter by a single value, an interval likely to include the parameter is given. Thus, Confidence intervals are used to indicate the reliability of an estimate.

Interval estimation

In statistics, Interval estimation is the use of sample data to calculate an interval of possible values of an unknown population parameter, in contrast to point estimation, which is a single number. Neyman (1937) identified Interval estimation as distinct from point estimation (`estimation by unique estimate`). In doing so, he recognised that then-recent work quoting results in the form of an estimate plus-or-minus a standard deviation indicated that Interval estimation was actually the problem statisticians really had in mind.

Chapter 8. Statistical Inference: Estimation for Single Populations

Chapter 8. Statistical Inference: Estimation for Single Populations

The most prevalent forms of Interval estimation are:

· confidence intervals (a frequentist method); and

· credible intervals (a Bayesian method).

Other common approaches to Interval estimation, which are encompassed by statistical theory, are:

· Tolerance intervals

· Prediction intervals - used mainly in Regression Analysis

There is a third approach to statistical inference, namely fiducial inference, that also considers Interval estimation.

Score

In statistics, the Score or Score function is the partial derivative, with respect to some parameter θ, of the logarithm (commonly the natural logarithm) of the likelihood function. If the observation is X and its likelihood is L(θ;X), then the Score V can be found through the chain rule:

$$V = \frac{\partial}{\partial \theta} \log L(\theta; X) = \frac{1}{L(\theta; X)} \frac{\partial L(\theta; X)}{\partial \theta}.$$

Note that V is a function of θ and the observation X, so that, in general, it is not a statistic. Note also that V indicates the sensitivity of L(θ;X) (its variation normalized by its value.)

Sample mean

The Sample mean or empirical mean and the sample covariance are statistics computed from a collection of data.

Chapter 8. Statistical Inference: Estimation for Single Populations

Chapter 8. Statistical Inference: Estimation for Single Populations

Given a random sample $\mathbf{x}_1, \ldots, \mathbf{x}_N$ from an n-dimensional random variable $\mathbf{X}$, the Sample mean is

$$\bar{\mathbf{x}} = \frac{1}{N} \sum_{k=1}^{N} \mathbf{x}_k.$$

In coordinates, writing the vectors as columns,

$$\mathbf{x}_k = \begin{bmatrix} x_{1k} \\ \vdots \\ x_{nk} \end{bmatrix}, \quad \bar{\mathbf{x}} = \begin{bmatrix} \bar{x}_1 \\ \vdots \\ \bar{x}_n \end{bmatrix},$$

the entries of the Sample mean are

$$\bar{x}_i = \frac{1}{N} \sum_{k=1}^{N} x_{ik}, \quad i = 1, \ldots, n.$$

The sample covariance of $\mathbf{x}_1, \ldots, \mathbf{x}_N$ is the n-by-n matrix $\mathbf{Q} = [q_{ij}]$ with the entries given by

$$q_{ij} = \frac{1}{N-1} \sum_{k=1}^{N} (x_{ik} - \bar{x}_i)(x_{jk} - \bar{x}_j)$$

Chapter 8. Statistical Inference: Estimation for Single Populations

Chapter 8. Statistical Inference: Estimation for Single Populations

The Sample mean and the sample covariance matrix are unbiased estimates of the mean and the covariance matrix of the random variable X. The reason why the sample covariance matrix has $N - 1$ in the denominator rather than N is essentially that the population mean E(X) is not known and is replaced by the Sample mean $\bar{x}$.

Sample size

The sample size of a statistical sample is the number of repeated measurements that constitute it. It is typically denoted n, and is a non-negative integer natural number.

ANOVA

In statistics, ANOVA is a collection of statistical models, and their associated procedures, in which the observed variance is partitioned into components due to different sources of variation. In its simplest form ANOVA provides a statistical test of whether or not the means of several groups are all equal, and therefore generalizes Student's two-sample t-test to more than two groups. ANOVAs are helpful because they possess a certain advantage over a two-sample t-test. Doing multiple two-sample t-tests would result in a largely increased chance of committing a type I error. For this reason, ANOVAs are useful in comparing three or more means.
There are three conceptual classes of such models:

· Fixed-effects models assume that the data came from normal populations which may differ only in their means. (Model 1)

· Random effects models assume that the data describe a hierarchy of different populations whose differences are constrained by the hierarchy. (Model 2)

· Mixed-effect models describe the situations where both fixed and random effects are present. (Model 3)

Random sampling

In random sampling every combination of items from the frame, or stratum, has a known probability of occurring, but these probabilities are not necessarily equal. With any form of sampling there is a risk that the sample may not adequately represent the population but with random sampling there is a large body of statistical theory which quantifies the risk and thus enables an appropriate sample size to be chosen.

Systematic sample

A systematic sample is a statistical method involving the selection of a specific interval element from a sampling frame. Using this procedure each element in the population has a known and equal probability of selection. This makes it functionally similar to simple random sampling.

Chapter 8. Statistical Inference: Estimation for Single Populations

Chapter 8. Statistical Inference: Estimation for Single Populations

Student t distribution	The Student t distribution is a probability distribution that arises in the problem of estimating the mean of a normally distributed population when the sample size is small. It is the basis of the popular Student's t-tests for the statistical significance of the difference between two sample means, and for confidence intervals for the difference between two population means.
Degrees of freedom	In statistics, the number of degrees of freedom is the number of values in the final calculation of a statistic that are free to vary. Estimates of statistical parameters can be based upon different amounts of information or data. The number of independent pieces of information that go into the estimate of a parameter is called the degrees of freedom.
Population variance	If $\mu = E(X)$ is the expected value (mean) of the random variable X, then the population variance is $var(X) = E((X - \mu)^2)$.
Variance	In probability theory and statistics, the Variance is used as one of several descriptors of a distribution. It describes how far values lie from the mean. In particular, the Variance is one of the moments of a distribution.
Chi-square distribution	In probability theory and statistics, the Chi-square distribution with k degrees of freedom is the distribution of a sum of the squares of k independent standard normal random variables. It is one of the most widely used probability distributions in inferential statistics, e.g. in hypothesis testing, or in construction of confidence intervals. The best-known situations in which the Chi-square distribution is used are the common chi-square tests for goodness of fit of an observed distribution to a theoretical one, and of the independence of two criteria of classification of qualitative data. Many other statistical tests also lead to a use of this distribution, like Friedman's analysis of variance by ranks. If X_1, â€¦, X_k are independent, standard normal random variables, then the sum of their squares $$Q = \sum_{i=1}^{k} X_i^2$$

Chapter 8. Statistical Inference: Estimation for Single Populations

Chapter 8. Statistical Inference: Estimation for Single Populations

is distributed according to the Chi-square distribution with k degrees of freedom. This is usually denoted as

$$Q \sim \chi^2(k) \quad \text{or} \quad Q \sim \chi_k^2$$

The Chi-square distribution has one parameter: k -- a positive integer that specifies the number of degrees of freedom (i.e. the number of X_i`s)

Central limit theorem

In probability theory, the Central limit theorem states conditions under which the mean of a sufficiently large number of independent random variables, each with finite mean and variance, will be approximately normally distributed (Rice 1995). The Central limit theorem also requires the random variables to be identically distributed, unless certain conditions are met. Since real-world quantities are often the balanced sum of many unobserved random events, this theorem provides a partial explanation for the prevalence of the normal probability distribution.

Sample proportion

Sample proportion is the fraction of samples which were successes. The proportion of successes in the sample is also a random variable.

Chapter 8. Statistical Inference: Estimation for Single Populations

Chapter 9. Statistical Inference: Hypothesis Testing for Single Populations

Statistical inference	Statistical inference is the process of making conclusions using data that is subject to random variation, for example, observational errors or sampling variation. More substantially, the terms Statistical inference, statistical induction and inferential statistics are used to describe systems of procedures that can be used to draw conclusions from datasets arising from systems affected by random variation. Initial requirements of such a system of procedures for inference and induction are that the system should produce reasonable answers when applied to well-defined situations and that it should be general enough to be applied across a range of situations.
Tree diagram	In mathematics and statistical methods, a Tree diagram is used to determine the probability of getting specific results where the possibilities are nested.
Chi-square test	`Chi-square test` also known as Pearson`s Chi-square test. A Chi-square test is any statistical hypothesis test in which the sampling distribution of the test statistic is a chi-square distribution when the null hypothesis is true, or any in which this is asymptotically true, meaning that the sampling distribution (if the null hypothesis is true) can be made to approximate a chi-square distribution as closely as desired by making the sample size large enough. Some examples of chi-squared tests where the chi-square distribution is only approximately valid: · Pearson`s Chi-square test, also known as the chi-square goodness-of-fit test or Chi-square test for independence. When mentioned without any modifiers or without other precluding context, this test is usually understood .  · Yates` Chi-square test, also known as Yates` correction for continuity. · Mantel-Haenszel Chi-square test. · Linear-by-linear association Chi-square test. · The portmanteau test in time-series analysis, testing for the presence of autocorrelation

Chapter 9. Statistical Inference: Hypothesis Testing for Single Populations

Chapter 9. Statistical Inference: Hypothesis Testing for Single Populations

	· Likelihood-ratio tests in general statistical modelling, for testing whether there is evidence of the need to move from a simple model to a more complicated one (where the simple model is nested within the complicated one).
Two-tailed test	The Two-tailed test is a statistical test used in inference, in which a given statistical hypothesis , H_0 (null hypothesis) will be rejected when the value of the statistic is either sufficiently small or sufficiently large. The test is named after the `tail` of data under the far left and far right of a bell-shaped normal data distribution, or bell curve. However, the terminology is extended to tests relating to distributions other than normal.
Runs test	The Runs test is a non-parametric test that checks a randomness hypothesis for a two-valued data sequence. More precisely, it can be used to test the hypothesis that the elements of the sequence are mutually independent. A `run` of a sequence is a maximal non-empty segment of the sequence consisting of adjacent equal elements. For example, the sequence `++++---+++--++++++----` consists of six runs, three of which consist of +'s and the others of –'s. If +s and –s alternate randomly, the number of runs in a sequence of length N for which it is given that there are N_+ occurrences of + and N_- occurrences of - (so $N = N_+ + N_-$) is a random variable whose conditional distribution - given the observation of N_+ and N_- - is approximately normal with:

$$\cdot \text{ mean} \quad \mu = \frac{2\,N_+\,N_-}{N} + 1,$$

$$\cdot \text{ variance} \quad \sigma^2 = \frac{2\,N_+\,N_-\,(2\,N_+\,N_- - N)}{N^2\,(N-1)} = \frac{(\mu-1)(\mu-2)}{N-1}.$$

Two-tailed Hypothesis	Two-tailed hypothesis refers when the prediction does not specify a direction. The important thing to remember about stating hypotheses is that you formulate your prediction and that a second hypothesis is formulated and incorporates all possible alternative outcomes for the case.
Rejection region	If the test statistic is inside the critical region, then our conclusion is one of the following: The hypothesis is incorrect, therefore reject the null hypothesis. (Therefore the critical region is sometimes called the rejection region). An event of probability less than or equal to alpha has occurred.

Chapter 9. Statistical Inference: Hypothesis Testing for Single Populations

Chapter 9. Statistical Inference: Hypothesis Testing for Single Populations

Critical value

In differential topology, a Critical value of a differentiable function $f: M \to N$ between differentiable manifolds is the value $f(x) \in N$ of a critical point $x \in M$.

The basic result on Critical values is Sard's lemma. The set of Critical values can be quite irregular; but in Morse theory it becomes important to consider real-valued functions on a manifold M, such that the set of Critical values is in fact finite.

Type I error

In statistics, the terms type I error (also, α error, false alarm rate (FAR) or false positive) and type II error (β error) are used to describe possible errors made in a statistical decision process. In 1928, Jerzy Neyman (1894-1981) and Egon Pearson (1895-1980), both eminent statisticians, discussed the problems associated with `deciding whether or not a particular sample may be judged as likely to have been randomly drawn from a certain population` (1928/1967, p.1): and identified `two sources of error`, namely:
Type I (α): reject the null hypothesis when the null hypothesis is true, and
Type II (β): fail to reject the null hypothesis when the null hypothesis is false

In 1930, they elaborated on these two sources of error, remarking that `in testing hypotheses two considerations must be kept in view, (1) we must be able to reduce the chance of rejecting a true hypothesis to as low a value as desired; (2) the test must be so devised that it will reject the hypothesis tested when it is likely to be false.`

Scientists recognize two different sorts of error:

· Statistical error: the difference between a computed, estimated, or measured value and the true, specified, or theoretically correct value that is caused by random, and inherently unpredictable fluctuations in the measurement apparatus or the system being studied.

· Systematic error: the difference between a computed, estimated, or measured value and the true, specified, or theoretically correct value that is caused by non-random fluctuations from an unknown source , and which, once identified, can usually be eliminated.

Chapter 9. Statistical Inference: Hypothesis Testing for Single Populations

Chapter 9. Statistical Inference: Hypothesis Testing for Single Populations

Statisticians speak of two significant sorts of statistical error. The context is that there is a `null hypothesis` which corresponds to a presumed default `state of nature`, e.g., that an individual is free of disease, that an accused is innocent, or that a potential login candidate is not authorized.

Type II error

In statistics, the terms type I error (also, α error, false alarm rate (FAR) or false positive) and Type II error (β error) are used to describe possible errors made in a statistical decision process. In 1928, Jerzy Neyman (1894-1981) and Egon Pearson (1895-1980), both eminent statisticians, discussed the problems associated with `deciding whether or not a particular sample may be judged as likely to have been randomly drawn from a certain population` (1928/1967, p.1): and identified `two sources of error`, namely:

Type I (α): reject the null hypothesis when the null hypothesis is true, and
Type II (β): fail to reject the null hypothesis when the null hypothesis is false

In 1930, they elaborated on these two sources of error, remarking that `in testing hypotheses two considerations must be kept in view, (1) we must be able to reduce the chance of rejecting a true hypothesis to as low a value as desired; (2) the test must be so devised that it will reject the hypothesis tested when it is likely to be false.`

Scientists recognize two different sorts of error:

· Statistical error: the difference between a computed, estimated, or measured value and the true, specified, or theoretically correct value that is caused by random, and inherently unpredictable fluctuations in the measurement apparatus or the system being studied.

· Systematic error: the difference between a computed, estimated, or measured value and the true, specified, or theoretically correct value that is caused by non-random fluctuations from an unknown source , and which, once identified, can usually be eliminated.

Statisticians speak of two significant sorts of statistical error. The context is that there is a `null hypothesis` which corresponds to a presumed default `state of nature`, e.g., that an individual is free of disease, that an accused is innocent, or that a potential login candidate is not authorized.

Mean

In statistics, mean has two related meanings:

Chapter 9. Statistical Inference: Hypothesis Testing for Single Populations

Chapter 9. Statistical Inference: Hypothesis Testing for Single Populations

· the arithmetic mean .

· the expected value of a random variable, which is also called the population mean.
It is sometimes stated that the `mean` means average. This is incorrect if `mean` is taken in the specific sense of `arithmetic mean` as there are different types of averages: the mean, median, and mode.

Sample

In statistics, a Sample is a subset of a population. Typically, the population is very large, making a census or a complete enumeration of all the values in the population impractical or impossible. The Sample represents a subset of manageable size.

Sample mean

The Sample mean or empirical mean and the sample covariance are statistics computed from a collection of data.

Given a random sample $\mathbf{X}_1, \ldots, \mathbf{X}_N$ from an n -dimensional random variable $\mathbf{X}$, the Sample mean is

$$\bar{\mathbf{X}} = \frac{1}{N} \sum_{k=1}^{N} \mathbf{X}_k .$$

In coordinates, writing the vectors as columns,

$$\mathbf{X}_k = \begin{bmatrix} x_{1k} \\ \vdots \\ x_{nk} \end{bmatrix}, \quad \bar{\mathbf{X}} = \begin{bmatrix} \bar{x}_1 \\ \vdots \\ \bar{x}_n \end{bmatrix},$$

the entries of the Sample mean are

Chapter 9. Statistical Inference: Hypothesis Testing for Single Populations

Chapter 9. Statistical Inference: Hypothesis Testing for Single Populations

$$\bar{x}_i = \frac{1}{N} \sum_{k=1}^{N} x_{ik}, \quad i = 1, \ldots, n.$$

The sample covariance of $\mathbf{X}_1, \ldots, \mathbf{X}_N$ is the n-by-n matrix $\mathbf{Q} = [q_{ij}]$ with the entries given by

$$q_{ij} = \frac{1}{N-1} \sum_{k=1}^{N} (x_{ik} - \bar{x}_i)(x_{jk} - \bar{x}_j)$$

The Sample mean and the sample covariance matrix are unbiased estimates of the mean and the covariance matrix of the random variable $\mathbf{X}$. The reason why the sample covariance matrix has $N-1$ in the denominator rather than N is essentially that the population mean E(X) is not known and is replaced by the Sample mean $\bar{x}$.

Mann-Whitney U test	In statistics, the Mann-Whitney U test is a non-parametric test for assessing whether two independent samples of observations come from the same distribution. It is one of the best-known non-parametric significance tests. It was proposed initially by Frank Wilcoxon in 1945, for equal sample sizes, and extended to arbitrary sample sizes and in other ways by H. B. Mann and Whitney (1947).
Power	The Power of a statistical test is the probability that the test will reject a false null hypothesis (i.e. that it will not make a Type II error). As Power increases, the chances of a Type II error decrease. The probability of a Type II error is referred to as the false negative rate (β). Therefore Power is equal to $1 - \beta$.
P-value	In statistical significance testing, the P-value is the probability of obtaining a test statistic at least as extreme as the one that was actually observed, assuming that the null hypothesis is true. A closely related concept is the E-value, which is the average number of times in multiple testing that one expects to obtain a test statistic at least as extreme as the one that was actually observed, assuming that the null hypothesis is true. When the tests are statistically independent the E-value is the product of the number of tests and the P-value.

Chapter 9. Statistical Inference: Hypothesis Testing for Single Populations

Chapter 9. Statistical Inference: Hypothesis Testing for Single Populations

Poisson distribution	In probability theory and statistics, the Poisson distribution is a discrete probability distribution that expresses the probability of a number of events occurring in a fixed period of time if these events occur with a known average rate and independently of the time since the last event.

The distribution was first introduced by Siméon-Denis Poisson (1781-1840) and published, together with his probability theory, in 1838 in his work Recherches sur la probabilité des jugements en matière criminelle et en matière civile . The work focused on certain random variables N that count, among other things, the number of discrete occurrences (sometimes called `arrivals`) that take place during a time-interval of given length. |
| Null hypothesis | The practice of science involves formulating and testing hypotheses, assertions that are falsifiable using a test of observed data. The Null hypothesis typically proposes a general or default position, such as that there is no relationship between two measured phenomena, or that a potential treatment has no effect. The term was originally coined by English geneticist and statistician Ronald Fisher. It is typically paired with a second hypothesis, the alternative hypothesis, which asserts a particular relationship between the phenomena. Jerzy Neyman and Egon Pearson formalized the notion of the alternative. The alternative need not be the logical negation of the Null hypothesis and is the predicted hypothesis you would get from the experiment. The use of alternative hypotheses was not part of Fisher`s formulation, but became standard. |
| Decision rule | In decision theory, a Decision rule is a function which maps an observation to an appropriate action. Decision rules play an important role in the theory of statistics and economics, and are closely related to the concept of a strategy in game theory.

In order to evaluate the usefulness of a Decision rule, it is necessary to have a loss function detailing the outcome of each action under different states.

Given an observable random variable X over the probability space $(\mathcal{X}, \Sigma, P_\theta)$, determined by a parameter $\theta \in \Theta$, and a set A of possible actions, a (deterministic) Decision rule is a function $\delta : \mathcal{X} \to A$. |

Chapter 9. Statistical Inference: Hypothesis Testing for Single Populations

Chapter 9. Statistical Inference: Hypothesis Testing for Single Populations

ANOVA	In statistics, ANOVA is a collection of statistical models, and their associated procedures, in which the observed variance is partitioned into components due to different sources of variation. In its simplest form ANOVA provides a statistical test of whether or not the means of several groups are all equal, and therefore generalizes Student's two-sample t-test to more than two groups. ANOVAs are helpful because they possess a certain advantage over a two-sample t-test. Doing multiple two-sample t-tests would result in a largely increased chance of committing a type I error. For this reason, ANOVAs are useful in comparing three or more means. There are three conceptual classes of such models: · Fixed-effects models assume that the data came from normal populations which may differ only in their means. (Model 1) · Random effects models assume that the data describe a hierarchy of different populations whose differences are constrained by the hierarchy. (Model 2) · Mixed-effect models describe the situations where both fixed and random effects are present. (Model 3)
Random sampling	In random sampling every combination of items from the frame, or stratum, has a known probability of occurring, but these probabilities are not necessarily equal. With any form of sampling there is a risk that the sample may not adequately represent the population but with random sampling there is a large body of statistical theory which quantifies the risk and thus enables an appropriate sample size to be chosen.
Systematic sample	A systematic sample is a statistical method involving the selection of a specific interval element from a sampling frame. Using this procedure each element in the population has a known and equal probability of selection. This makes it functionally similar to simple random sampling.
Realization	In probability and statistics, a Realization of a random variable is the value that is actually observed (what actually happened.) The random variable itself should be thought of as the process how the observation comes about. Statistical quantities computed from realizations without deploying a statistical model are often called `empirical`, as in empirical distribution function or empirical probability.
Population variance	If $\mu = E(X)$ is the expected value (mean) of the random variable X, then the population variance is $var(X) = E((X - \mu)^2)$.

Chapter 9. Statistical Inference: Hypothesis Testing for Single Populations

Chapter 9. Statistical Inference: Hypothesis Testing for Single Populations

Variance

In probability theory and statistics, the Variance is used as one of several descriptors of a distribution. It describes how far values lie from the mean. In particular, the Variance is one of the moments of a distribution.

Sample size

The sample size of a statistical sample is the number of repeated measurements that constitute it. It is typically denoted n, and is a non-negative integer natural number.

Central limit theorem

In probability theory, the Central limit theorem states conditions under which the mean of a sufficiently large number of independent random variables, each with finite mean and variance, will be approximately normally distributed (Rice 1995). The Central limit theorem also requires the random variables to be identically distributed, unless certain conditions are met. Since real-world quantities are often the balanced sum of many unobserved random events, this theorem provides a partial explanation for the prevalence of the normal probability distribution.

Friedman test

The Friedman test is a non-parametric statistical test developed by the U.S. economist Milton Friedman. Similar to the parametric repeated measures ANOVA, it is used to detect differences in treatments across multiple test attempts. The procedure involves ranking each row (or block) together, then considering the values of ranks by columns. Applicable to complete block designs, it is thus a special case of the Durbin test.

Classic examples of use are:

· n wine judges rate k different wines. Are any wines ranked consistently higher or lower than the others?

· n wines are rated by k different judges. Are the judges ratings consistent with each other?

· n welders use k welding torches, and the ensuing welds were rated on quality. Do any of the torches produce consistently better or worse welds?

Chapter 9. Statistical Inference: Hypothesis Testing for Single Populations

Chapter 10. Statistical Inferences About Two Populations

Statistical inference	Statistical inference is the process of making conclusions using data that is subject to random variation, for example, observational errors or sampling variation. More substantially, the terms Statistical inference, statistical induction and inferential statistics are used to describe systems of procedures that can be used to draw conclusions from datasets arising from systems affected by random variation. Initial requirements of such a system of procedures for inference and induction are that the system should produce reasonable answers when applied to well-defined situations and that it should be general enough to be applied across a range of situations.
Confidence interval	In statistics, a Confidence interval is a particular kind of interval estimate of a population parameter. Instead of estimating the parameter by a single value, an interval likely to include the parameter is given. Thus, Confidence intervals are used to indicate the reliability of an estimate.
Sample	In statistics, a Sample is a subset of a population. Typically, the population is very large, making a census or a complete enumeration of all the values in the population impractical or impossible. The Sample represents a subset of manageable size.
Estimator	In statistics, an Estimator or point estimate is a statistic (that is, a measurable function of the data) that is used to infer the value of an unknown parameter in a statistical model. The parameter being estimated is sometimes called the estimand. It can be either finite-dimensional , or infinite-dimensional (semi-nonparametric and non-parametric models).
Tree diagram	In mathematics and statistical methods, a Tree diagram is used to determine the probability of getting specific results where the possibilities are nested.
Mann-Whitney U test	In statistics, the Mann-Whitney U test is a non-parametric test for assessing whether two independent samples of observations come from the same distribution. It is one of the best-known non-parametric significance tests. It was proposed initially by Frank Wilcoxon in 1945, for equal sample sizes, and extended to arbitrary sample sizes and in other ways by H. B. Mann and Whitney (1947).
Mean	In statistics, mean has two related meanings: · the arithmetic mean . · the expected value of a random variable, which is also called the population mean.

Chapter 10. Statistical Inferences About Two Populations

Chapter 10. Statistical Inferences About Two Populations

	It is sometimes stated that the `mean` means average. This is incorrect if `mean` is taken in the specific sense of `arithmetic mean` as there are different types of averages: the mean, median, and mode.
ANOVA	In statistics, ANOVA is a collection of statistical models, and their associated procedures, in which the observed variance is partitioned into components due to different sources of variation. In its simplest form ANOVA provides a statistical test of whether or not the means of several groups are all equal, and therefore generalizes Student's two-sample t-test to more than two groups. ANOVAs are helpful because they possess a certain advantage over a two-sample t-test. Doing multiple two-sample t-tests would result in a largely increased chance of committing a type I error. For this reason, ANOVAs are useful in comparing three or more means. There are three conceptual classes of such models: · Fixed-effects models assume that the data came from normal populations which may differ only in their means. (Model 1) · Random effects models assume that the data describe a hierarchy of different populations whose differences are constrained by the hierarchy. (Model 2) · Mixed-effect models describe the situations where both fixed and random effects are present. (Model 3)
Factorial design	In statistics, a full Factorial design is an experiment whose design consists of two or more factors, each with discrete possible values or `levels`, and whose experimental units take on all possible combinations of these levels across all such factors. A full Factorial design may also be called a fully crossed design. Such an experiment allows studying the effect of each factor on the response variable, as well as the effects of interactions between factors on the response variable.
Interaction	Interaction is a kind of action that occurs as two or more objects have an effect upon one another. The idea of a two-way effect is essential in the concept of Interaction, as opposed to a one-way causal effect. A closely related term is interconnectivity, which deals with the Interactions of Interactions within systems: combinations of many simple Interactions can lead to surprising emergent phenomena.

Chapter 10. Statistical Inferences About Two Populations

Chapter 10. Statistical Inferences About Two Populations

Regression analysis

In statistics, Regression analysis includes any techniques for modeling and analyzing several variables, when the focus is on the relationship between a dependent variable and one or more independent variables. More specifically, Regression analysis helps us understand how the typical value of the dependent variable changes when any one of the independent variables is varied, while the other independent variables are held fixed. Most commonly, Regression analysis estimates the conditional expectation of the dependent variable given the independent variables -- that is, the average value of the dependent variable when the independent variables are held fixed.

Random sampling

In random sampling every combination of items from the frame, or stratum, has a known probability of occurring, but these probabilities are not necessarily equal. With any form of sampling there is a risk that the sample may not adequately represent the population but with random sampling there is a large body of statistical theory which quantifies the risk and thus enables an appropriate sample size to be chosen.

Systematic sample

A systematic sample is a statistical method involving the selection of a specific interval element from a sampling frame. Using this procedure each element in the population has a known and equal probability of selection. This makes it functionally similar to simple random sampling.

Central tendency

In statistics, the term Central tendency relates to the way in which quantitative data tend to cluster around some value. A measure of Central tendency is any of a number of ways of specifying this `central value`. In practical statistical analyses, the terms are often used before one has chosen even a preliminary form of analysis: thus an initial objective might be to `choose an appropriate measure of Central tendency`.

Poisson distribution

In probability theory and statistics, the Poisson distribution is a discrete probability distribution that expresses the probability of a number of events occurring in a fixed period of time if these events occur with a known average rate and independently of the time since the last event.

The distribution was first introduced by Siméon-Denis Poisson (1781-1840) and published, together with his probability theory, in 1838 in his work Recherches sur la probabilité des jugements en matière criminelle et en matière civile . The work focused on certain random variables N that count, among other things, the number of discrete occurrences (sometimes called `arrivals`) that take place during a time-interval of given length.

Chapter 10. Statistical Inferences About Two Populations

Chapter 10. Statistical Inferences About Two Populations

Central limit theorem	In probability theory, the Central limit theorem states conditions under which the mean of a sufficiently large number of independent random variables, each with finite mean and variance, will be approximately normally distributed (Rice 1995). The Central limit theorem also requires the random variables to be identically distributed, unless certain conditions are met. Since real-world quantities are often the balanced sum of many unobserved random events, this theorem provides a partial explanation for the prevalence of the normal probability distribution.
Correlation	In statistics, Correlation indicates the strength and direction of a relationship between two random variables. The commonest use refers to a linear relationship, but the concept of nonlinear Correlation is also used. In general statistical usage, Correlation or co-relation refers to the departure of two random variables from independence.
Rank correlation	In statistics, Rank correlation is the study of relationships between different rankings on the same set of items. A Rank correlation coefficient measures the correspondence between two rankings and assesses its significance.

Two of the more popular Rank correlation statistics are

· Spearman`s Rank correlation coefficient (Spearman`s ρ)

· Kendall`s tau Rank correlation coefficient (Kendall`s τ)
An increasing Rank correlation coefficient implies increasing agreement between rankings. The coefficient is inside the interval $[-1, 1]$ and assumes the value:

· -1 if the disagreement between the two rankings is perfect; one ranking is the reverse of the other.

· 0 if the rankings are completely independent.

· 1 if the agreement between the two rankings is perfect; the two rankings are the same.

Following the Diaconis reference below, a ranking can be seen as a permutation of a set of objects.

Population variance	If $\mu = E(X)$ is the expected value (mean) of the random variable X, then the population variance is $var(X) = E((X - \mu)^2)$.

Chapter 10. Statistical Inferences About Two Populations

Chapter 11. Analysis of Variance and Design of Experiments

ANOVA	In statistics, ANOVA is a collection of statistical models, and their associated procedures, in which the observed variance is partitioned into components due to different sources of variation. In its simplest form ANOVA provides a statistical test of whether or not the means of several groups are all equal, and therefore generalizes Student's two-sample t-test to more than two groups. ANOVAs are helpful because they possess a certain advantage over a two-sample t-test. Doing multiple two-sample t-tests would result in a largely increased chance of committing a type I error. For this reason, ANOVAs are useful in comparing three or more means. There are three conceptual classes of such models: · Fixed-effects models assume that the data came from normal populations which may differ only in their means. (Model 1) · Random effects models assume that the data describe a hierarchy of different populations whose differences are constrained by the hierarchy. (Model 2) · Mixed-effect models describe the situations where both fixed and random effects are present. (Model 3)
Variance	In probability theory and statistics, the Variance is used as one of several descriptors of a distribution. It describes how far values lie from the mean. In particular, the Variance is one of the moments of a distribution.
Design of experiments	In general usage, Design of experiments or experimental design is the design of any information-gathering exercises where variation is present, whether under the full control of the experimenter or not. However, in statistics, these terms are usually used for controlled experiments. Other types of study, and their design, are discussed in the articles on opinion polls and statistical surveys (which are types of observational study), natural experiments and quasi-experiments (for example, quasi-experimental design). In the Design of experiments, the experimenter is often interested in the effect of some process or intervention (the `treatment`) on some objects (the `experimental units`), which may be people, parts of people, groups of people, plants, animals, materials, etc. Design of experiments is thus a discipline that has very broad application across all the natural and social sciences.
Independent variable	The terms `dependent variable` and `Independent variable` are used in similar but subtly different ways in mathematics and statistics as part of the standard terminology in those subjects. They are used to distinguish between two types of quantities being considered, separating them into those available at the start of a process and those being created by it, where the latter (dependent variables) are dependent on the former (Independent variables).

Chapter 11. Analysis of Variance and Design of Experiments

Chapter 11. Analysis of Variance and Design of Experiments

	The Independent variable is typically the variable being manipulated or changed and the dependent variable is the observed result of the Independent variable being manipulated.
Completely randomized designs	In the design of experiments, Completely randomized designs are for studying the effects of one primary factor without the need to take other nuisance variables into account The experiment compares the values of a response variable based on the different levels of that primary factor. For Completely randomized designs, the levels of the primary factor are randomly assigned to the experimental units.
Tree diagram	In mathematics and statistical methods, a Tree diagram is used to determine the probability of getting specific results where the possibilities are nested.
Dependent variable	The terms `dependent variable` and `independent variable` are used in similar but subtly different ways in mathematics and statistics as part of the standard terminology in those subjects. They are used to distinguish between two types of quantities being considered, separating them into those available at the start of a process and those being created by it, where the latter (dependent variables) are dependent on the former (independent variables). The independent variable is typically the variable representing the value being manipulated or changed and the dependent variable is the observed result of the independent variable being manipulated.
One-way ANOVA	In statistics, One-way ANOVA is a technique used to compare means of two or more samples (using the F distribution). This technique can be used only for numerical data. The ANOVA tests the null hypothesis that samples in two or more groups are drawn from the same population. To do this, two estimates are made of the population variance. These estimates rely on various assumptions. The ANOVA produces an F statistic, the ratio of the variance calculated among the means to the variance within the samples. If the group means are drawn from the same population, the variance between the group means should be lower than the variance of the samples, following central limit theorem. A higher ratio therefore implies that the samples were drawn from different populations.
Mann-Whitney U test	In statistics, the Mann-Whitney U test is a non-parametric test for assessing whether two independent samples of observations come from the same distribution. It is one of the best-known non-parametric significance tests. It was proposed initially by Frank Wilcoxon in 1945, for equal sample sizes, and extended to arbitrary sample sizes and in other ways by H. B. Mann and Whitney (1947).

Chapter 11. Analysis of Variance and Design of Experiments

Chapter 11. Analysis of Variance and Design of Experiments

Random sampling	In random sampling every combination of items from the frame, or stratum, has a known probability of occurring, but these probabilities are not necessarily equal. With any form of sampling there is a risk that the sample may not adequately represent the population but with random sampling there is a large body of statistical theory which quantifies the risk and thus enables an appropriate sample size to be chosen.
Systematic sample	A systematic sample is a statistical method involving the selection of a specific interval element from a sampling frame. Using this procedure each element in the population has a known and equal probability of selection. This makes it functionally similar to simple random sampling.
Multiple comparisons	In statistics, the Multiple comparisons problem occurs when one considers a set, or family, of statistical inferences simultaneously. Errors in inference, including confidence intervals that fail to include their corresponding population parameters, or hypothesis tests that incorrectly reject the null hypothesis, are more likely to occur when one considers the family as a whole. Several statistical techniques have been developed to prevent this from happening, allowing significance levels for single and Multiple comparisons to be directly compared.
Post hoc comparisons	Multiple comparison procedures are commonly used after obtaining a significant ANOVA F-test; called post hoc comparisons. The significant ANOVA result suggests rejecting the global null hypothesis H_0 = "means are the same". Multiple comparison procedures are then used to determine which means are different from each other.
Mean	In statistics, mean has two related meanings: · the arithmetic mean . · the expected value of a random variable, which is also called the population mean. It is sometimes stated that the `mean` means average. This is incorrect if `mean` is taken in the specific sense of `arithmetic mean` as there are different types of averages: the mean, median, and mode.
Mean square error	In statistics, the Mean square error of an estimator is one of many ways to quantify the difference between an estimator and the true value of the quantity being estimated. Mean square error is a risk function, corresponding to the expected value of the squared error loss or quadratic loss. Mean square error measures the average of the square of the `error.` The error is the amount by which the estimator differs from the quantity to be estimated.

Chapter 11. Analysis of Variance and Design of Experiments

Chapter 11. Analysis of Variance and Design of Experiments

Pairwise comparison	Pairwise comparison generally refers to any process of comparing entities in pairs to judge which of each pair is preferred or has a greater amount of some quantitative property. The method of Pairwise comparison is used in the scientific study of preferences, attitudes, voting systems, social choice, public choice, and multiagent AI systems. In psychology literature, it is often referred to as paired comparison.
Confounding variable	In statistics, a confounding variable (also confounding factor, lurking variable, a confound) is an extraneous variable in a statistical model that correlates (positively or negatively) with both the dependent variable and the independent variable. The methodologies of scientific studies therefore need to control for these factors to avoid a type 1 error; an erroneous `false positive` conclusion that the dependent variables are in a causal relationship with the independent variable. Such a relation between two observed variables is termed a spurious relationship.
Randomized block design	In general terms, we can define that a randomized block design as a design in which k treatments are compared within each of b blocks. Each block contains k matched experimental units and the k treatments are randomly assigned, one to each of the units within each block.
Repeated measures design	A Repeated measures design is a longitudinal study, usually a controlled experiment but sometimes an observational study (often referred to as a longitudinal or panel study). Randomized, controlled, crossover experiments are especially important in health-care. In a randomized clinical trial, the subjects are randomly assigned treatments.
Sum of squares	Sum of squares is a concept that permeates much of inferential statistics and descriptive statistics. More properly, it is the sum of squared deviations. Mathematically, it is an unscaled, or unadjusted measure of dispersion (also called variability). When scaled for the number of degrees of freedom, it estimates the variance, or spread of the observations about their mean value. The distance from any point in a collection of data, to the mean of the data, is the deviation. This can be written as $X_i - \overline{X}$, where X_i is the ith data point, and $\overline{X}$ is the estimate of the mean. If all such deviations are squared, then summed, as in $\sum_{i=1}^{n} \left(X_i - \overline{X} \right)^2$, we have the `Sum of squares` for these data.
Chi-square test	`Chi-square test` also known as Pearson`s Chi-square test.

Chapter 11. Analysis of Variance and Design of Experiments

Chapter 11. Analysis of Variance and Design of Experiments

A Chi-square test is any statistical hypothesis test in which the sampling distribution of the test statistic is a chi-square distribution when the null hypothesis is true, or any in which this is asymptotically true, meaning that the sampling distribution (if the null hypothesis is true) can be made to approximate a chi-square distribution as closely as desired by making the sample size large enough.

Some examples of chi-squared tests where the chi-square distribution is only approximately valid:

· Pearson`s Chi-square test, also known as the chi-square goodness-of-fit test or Chi-square test for independence. When mentioned without any modifiers or without other precluding context, this test is usually understood .

· Yates` Chi-square test, also known as Yates` correction for continuity.

· Mantel-Haenszel Chi-square test.

· Linear-by-linear association Chi-square test.

· The portmanteau test in time-series analysis, testing for the presence of autocorrelation

· Likelihood-ratio tests in general statistical modelling, for testing whether there is evidence of the need to move from a simple model to a more complicated one (where the simple model is nested within the complicated one).

| Poisson distribution | In probability theory and statistics, the Poisson distribution is a discrete probability distribution that expresses the probability of a number of events occurring in a fixed period of time if these events occur with a known average rate and independently of the time since the last event. |

The distribution was first introduced by Siméon-Denis Poisson (1781-1840) and published, together with his probability theory, in 1838 in his work Recherches sur la probabilité des jugements en matière criminelle et en matière civile . The work focused on certain random variables N that count, among other things, the number of discrete occurrences (sometimes called `arrivals`) that take place during a time-interval of given length.

Chapter 11. Analysis of Variance and Design of Experiments

Chapter 11. Analysis of Variance and Design of Experiments

Factorial design	In statistics, a full Factorial design is an experiment whose design consists of two or more factors, each with discrete possible values or `levels`, and whose experimental units take on all possible combinations of these levels across all such factors. A full Factorial design may also be called a fully crossed design. Such an experiment allows studying the effect of each factor on the response variable, as well as the effects of interactions between factors on the response variable.
Two-way Analysis	Two-way analysis is the computation of two variances price and quantity variances for direct materials and direct labor and budget and volume variances for factory overhead.
Interaction	Interaction is a kind of action that occurs as two or more objects have an effect upon one another. The idea of a two-way effect is essential in the concept of Interaction, as opposed to a one-way causal effect. A closely related term is interconnectivity, which deals with the Interactions of Interactions within systems: combinations of many simple Interactions can lead to surprising emergent phenomena.
Correlation	In statistics, Correlation indicates the strength and direction of a relationship between two random variables. The commonest use refers to a linear relationship, but the concept of nonlinear Correlation is also used. In general statistical usage, Correlation or co-relation refers to the departure of two random variables from independence.
Rank correlation	In statistics, Rank correlation is the study of relationships between different rankings on the same set of items. A Rank correlation coefficient measures the correspondence between two rankings and assesses its significance.
	Two of the more popular Rank correlation statistics are
	· Spearman`s Rank correlation coefficient (Spearman`s ρ)
	· Kendall`s tau Rank correlation coefficient (Kendall`s τ)
	An increasing Rank correlation coefficient implies increasing agreement between rankings. The coefficient is inside the interval [−1, 1] and assumes the value:
	· −1 if the disagreement between the two rankings is perfect; one ranking is the reverse of the other.
	· 0 if the rankings are completely independent.

Chapter 11. Analysis of Variance and Design of Experiments

Chapter 11. Analysis of Variance and Design of Experiments

· 1 if the agreement between the two rankings is perfect; the two rankings are the same.

Following the Diaconis reference below, a ranking can be seen as a permutation of a set of objects.

Chapter 11. Analysis of Variance and Design of Experiments

Chapter 12. Simple Regression Analysis and Correlation

Regression analysis

In statistics, Regression analysis includes any techniques for modeling and analyzing several variables, when the focus is on the relationship between a dependent variable and one or more independent variables. More specifically, Regression analysis helps us understand how the typical value of the dependent variable changes when any one of the independent variables is varied, while the other independent variables are held fixed. Most commonly, Regression analysis estimates the conditional expectation of the dependent variable given the independent variables -- that is, the average value of the dependent variable when the independent variables are held fixed.

Correlation

In statistics, Correlation indicates the strength and direction of a relationship between two random variables. The commonest use refers to a linear relationship, but the concept of nonlinear Correlation is also used. In general statistical usage, Correlation or co-relation refers to the departure of two random variables from independence.

Pearson correlation

In statistics, Pearson correlation is a measure of the correlation of two variables X and Y measured on the same object or organism, that is, a measure of the tendency of the variables to increase or decrease together. It is defined as the sum of the products of the standard scores of the two measures divided by the degrees of freedom:

$$r = \frac{\Sum z_x z_y}{n-1}$$

Note that this formula assumes the Z scores are calculated using standard deviations which are calculated using $n - 1$ in the denominator.

The result obtained is equivalent to dividing the covariance between the two variables by the product of their standard deviations.

Coefficient of determination

In statistics, the Coefficient of determination, R^2 is used in the context of statistical models whose main purpose is the prediction of future outcomes on the basis of other related information. It is the proportion of variability in a data set that is accounted for by the statistical model. It provides a measure of how well future outcomes are likely to be predicted by the model.

There are several different definitions of R^2 which are only sometimes equivalent. One class of such cases includes that of linear regression. In this case, R^2 is simply the square of the sample correlation coefficient between the outcomes and their predicted values, or in the case of simple linear regression, between the outcome and the values being used for prediction. In such cases, the values vary from 0 to 1. Important cases where the computational definition of R^2 can yield negative values, depending on the definition used, arise where the predictions which are being compared to the corresponding outcome have not derived from a model-fitting procedure using those data.

Chapter 12. Simple Regression Analysis and Correlation

Chapter 12. Simple Regression Analysis and Correlation

ANOVA	In statistics, ANOVA is a collection of statistical models, and their associated procedures, in which the observed variance is partitioned into components due to different sources of variation. In its simplest form ANOVA provides a statistical test of whether or not the means of several groups are all equal, and therefore generalizes Student's two-sample t-test to more than two groups. ANOVAs are helpful because they possess a certain advantage over a two-sample t-test. Doing multiple two-sample t-tests would result in a largely increased chance of committing a type I error. For this reason, ANOVAs are useful in comparing three or more means. There are three conceptual classes of such models: · Fixed-effects models assume that the data came from normal populations which may differ only in their means. (Model 1) · Random effects models assume that the data describe a hierarchy of different populations whose differences are constrained by the hierarchy. (Model 2) · Mixed-effect models describe the situations where both fixed and random effects are present. (Model 3)
Dependent variable	The terms `dependent variable` and `independent variable` are used in similar but subtly different ways in mathematics and statistics as part of the standard terminology in those subjects. They are used to distinguish between two types of quantities being considered, separating them into those available at the start of a process and those being created by it, where the latter (dependent variables) are dependent on the former (independent variables). The independent variable is typically the variable representing the value being manipulated or changed and the dependent variable is the observed result of the independent variable being manipulated.
Independent variable	The terms `dependent variable` and `Independent variable` are used in similar but subtly different ways in mathematics and statistics as part of the standard terminology in those subjects. They are used to distinguish between two types of quantities being considered, separating them into those available at the start of a process and those being created by it, where the latter (dependent variables) are dependent on the former (Independent variables). The Independent variable is typically the variable being manipulated or changed and the dependent variable is the observed result of the Independent variable being manipulated.

Chapter 12. Simple Regression Analysis and Correlation

Chapter 12. Simple Regression Analysis and Correlation

Scatter plot	A Scatter plot or scattergraph is a type of mathematical diagram using Cartesian coordinates to display values for two variables for a set of data.
	The data is displayed as a collection of points, each having the value of one variable determining the position on the horizontal axis and the value of the other variable determining the position on the vertical axis. This kind of plot is also called a scatter chart, scatter diagram and scatter graph.
Poisson distribution	In probability theory and statistics, the Poisson distribution is a discrete probability distribution that expresses the probability of a number of events occurring in a fixed period of time if these events occur with a known average rate and independently of the time since the last event.
	The distribution was first introduced by Siméon-Denis Poisson (1781-1840) and published, together with his probability theory, in 1838 in his work Recherches sur la probabilité des jugements en matière criminelle et en matière civile . The work focused on certain random variables N that count, among other things, the number of discrete occurrences (sometimes called `arrivals`) that take place during a time-interval of given length.
Regression line	Regression line is a line drawn through a scatterplot of two variables. The line is chosen so that it comes as close to the points as possible.
Least squares	The method of Least squares is a standard approach to the approximate solution of overdetermined systems, i.e. sets of equations in which there are more equations than unknowns. `Least squares` means that the overall solution minimizes the sum of the squares of the errors made in solving every single equation.
	The most important application is in data fitting. The best fit in the Least squares sense minimizes the sum of squared residuals, a residual being the difference between an observed value and the fitted value provided by a model.
Probabilistic model	A probabilistic model is a distribution model in which the data is modelled as random variables, the probability distribution of which depends on parameter values.
Line chart	A Line chart or line graph is a type of graph, which displays information as a series of data points connected by straight line segments. It is a basic type of chart common in many fields. It is an extension of a scatter graph, and is created by connecting a series of points that represent individual measurements with line segments.

Chapter 12. Simple Regression Analysis and Correlation

Chapter 12. Simple Regression Analysis and Correlation

Residual	Error is a misnomer; an error is the amount by which an observation differs from its expected value; the latter being based on the whole population from which the statistical unit was chosen randomly. A residual, on the other hand, is an observable estimate of the unobservable error.
Residual analysis	Residual analysis is a useful class of techniques for the evaluation of a fitted model. Checking the underlying assumptions is important since most linear regression estimators required a correctly specified regression function and independent distributed errors to be consistent.
Outlier	In statistics, an Outlier is an observation that is numerically distant from the rest of the data. Grubbs defined an Outlier as: An outlying observation, or Outlier, is one that appears to deviate markedly from other members of the sample in which it occurs. Outliers can occur by chance in any distribution, but they are often indicative either of measurement error or that the population has a heavy-tailed distribution.
Heteroscedastic	In statistics, a sequence of random variables is Heteroscedastic if the random variables have different variances. Suppose there is a sequence of random variables $\{Y_t\}_{t=1}^n$ and a sequence of vectors of random variables, $\{X_t\}_{t=1}^n$. In dealing with conditional expectations of Y_t given X_t, the sequence $\{Y_t\}_{t=1}^n$ is said to be heteroskedastic if the conditional variance of Y_t given X_t, changes with t. Some authors refer to this as conditional Heteroscedasticity to emphasize the fact that it is the sequence of conditional variance that changes and not the unconditional variance. In fact it is possible to observe conditional Heteroscedasticity even when dealing with a sequence of unconditional homoscedastic random variables, however, the opposite does not hold.
Variance	In probability theory and statistics, the Variance is used as one of several descriptors of a distribution. It describes how far values lie from the mean. In particular, the Variance is one of the moments of a distribution.
Standard error	The Standard error of a method of measurement or estimation is the standard deviation of the sampling distribution associated with the estimation method. The term may also be used to refer to an estimate of that standard deviation, derived from a particular sample used to compute the estimate.

Chapter 12. Simple Regression Analysis and Correlation

Chapter 12. Simple Regression Analysis and Correlation

For example, the sample mean is the usual estimator of a population mean. However, different samples drawn from that same population would in general have different values of the sample mean. The Standard error of the mean is the standard deviation of those sample means over all possible samples (of a given size) drawn from the population. Secondly, the Standard error of the mean can refer to an estimate of that standard deviation, computed from the sample of data being analysed at the time.

Sum of squares

Sum of squares is a concept that permeates much of inferential statistics and descriptive statistics. More properly, it is the sum of squared deviations. Mathematically, it is an unscaled, or unadjusted measure of dispersion (also called variability). When scaled for the number of degrees of freedom, it estimates the variance, or spread of the observations about their mean value.

The distance from any point in a collection of data, to the mean of the data, is the deviation. This can be written as $X_i - \overline{X}$, where X_i is the ith data point, and $\overline{X}$ is the estimate of the mean. If all such deviations are squared, then summed, as in $\sum_{i=1}^{n} \left(X_i - \overline{X} \right)^2$, we have the `Sum of squares` for these data.

Rank correlation

In statistics, Rank correlation is the study of relationships between different rankings on the same set of items. A Rank correlation coefficient measures the correspondence between two rankings and assesses its significance.

Two of the more popular Rank correlation statistics are

· Spearman`s Rank correlation coefficient (Spearman`s ρ)

· Kendall`s tau Rank correlation coefficient (Kendall`s τ)

An increasing Rank correlation coefficient implies increasing agreement between rankings. The coefficient is inside the interval [−1, 1] and assumes the value:

· −1 if the disagreement between the two rankings is perfect; one ranking is the reverse of the other.

· 0 if the rankings are completely independent.

Chapter 12. Simple Regression Analysis and Correlation

Chapter 12. Simple Regression Analysis and Correlation

	· 1 if the agreement between the two rankings is perfect; the two rankings are the same. Following the Diaconis reference below, a ranking can be seen as a permutation of a set of objects.
Range	In descriptive statistics, the Range is the length of the smallest interval which contains all the data. It is calculated by subtracting the smallest observation (sample minimum) from the greatest (sample maximum) and provides an indication of [statistical dispersion] It is measured in the same units as the data. Since it only depends on two of the observations, it is a poor and weak measure of dispersion except when the sample size is large.
Statistical dispersion	In statistics, Statistical dispersion is variability or spread in a variable or a probability distribution. Common examples of measures of Statistical dispersion are the variance, standard deviation and interquartile range. Dispersion is contrasted with location or central tendency, and together they are the most used properties of distributions.
Linear regression	In statistics, Linear regression is any approach to modeling the relationship between a scalar variable y and one or more variables denoted X. In Linear regression, models of the unknown parameters are estimated from the data using linear functions. Such models are called `linear models.` Most commonly, Linear regression refers to a model in which the conditional mean of y given the value of X is an affine function of X. Less commonly, Linear regression could refer to a model in which the median, or some other quantile of the conditional distribution of y given X is expressed as a linear function of X. Like all forms of regression analysis, Linear regression focuses on the conditional probability distribution of y given X, rather than on the joint probability distribution of y and X, which is the domain of multivariate analysis. Linear regression was the first type of regression analysis to be studied rigorously, and to be used extensively in practical applications.
Regression coefficient	The regression coefficient is the slope of the straight line that most closely relates two correlated variables.

Chapter 12. Simple Regression Analysis and Correlation

Chapter 12. Simple Regression Analysis and Correlation

Inverse relationship	An Inverse relationship or negative relationship is a mathematical relationship in which one variable, say y, decreases as another, say x, increases. For a linear (straight-line) relation, this can be expressed as y = a-bx, where -b is a constant value less than zero and a is a constant. For example, there is an Inverse relationship between education and unemployment -- that is, as education increases, the rate of unemployment decreases.
Random sampling	In random sampling every combination of items from the frame, or stratum, has a known probability of occurring, but these probabilities are not necessarily equal. With any form of sampling there is a risk that the sample may not adequately represent the population but with random sampling there is a large body of statistical theory which quantifies the risk and thus enables an appropriate sample size to be chosen.
Systematic sample	A systematic sample is a statistical method involving the selection of a specific interval element from a sampling frame. Using this procedure each element in the population has a known and equal probability of selection. This makes it functionally similar to simple random sampling.
Degrees of freedom	In statistics, the number of degrees of freedom is the number of values in the final calculation of a statistic that are free to vary. Estimates of statistical parameters can be based upon different amounts of information or data. The number of independent pieces of information that go into the estimate of a parameter is called the degrees of freedom.
Mean	In statistics, mean has two related meanings: · the arithmetic mean . · the expected value of a random variable, which is also called the population mean. It is sometimes stated that the `mean` means average. This is incorrect if `mean` is taken in the specific sense of `arithmetic mean` as there are different types of averages: the mean, median, and mode.
Confidence interval	In statistics, a Confidence interval is a particular kind of interval estimate of a population parameter. Instead of estimating the parameter by a single value, an interval likely to include the parameter is given. Thus, Confidence intervals are used to indicate the reliability of an estimate.

Chapter 12. Simple Regression Analysis and Correlation

Chapter 12. Simple Regression Analysis and Correlation

Friedman test	The Friedman test is a non-parametric statistical test developed by the U.S. economist Milton Friedman. Similar to the parametric repeated measures ANOVA, it is used to detect differences in treatments across multiple test attempts. The procedure involves ranking each row (or block) together, then considering the values of ranks by columns. Applicable to complete block designs, it is thus a special case of the Durbin test. Classic examples of use are: · n wine judges rate k different wines. Are any wines ranked consistently higher or lower than the others? · n wines are rated by k different judges. Are the judges ratings consistent with each other? · n welders use k welding torches, and the ensuing welds were rated on quality. Do any of the torches produce consistently better or worse welds?
Interval estimation	In statistics, Interval estimation is the use of sample data to calculate an interval of possible values of an unknown population parameter, in contrast to point estimation, which is a single number. Neyman (1937) identified Interval estimation as distinct from point estimation (`estimation by unique estimate`). In doing so, he recognised that then-recent work quoting results in the form of an estimate plus-or-minus a standard deviation indicated that Interval estimation was actually the problem statisticians really had in mind. The most prevalent forms of Interval estimation are: · confidence intervals (a frequentist method); and · credible intervals (a Bayesian method).

Chapter 12. Simple Regression Analysis and Correlation

Chapter 12. Simple Regression Analysis and Correlation

	Other common approaches to Interval estimation, which are encompassed by statistical theory, are: · Tolerance intervals · Prediction intervals - used mainly in Regression Analysis There is a third approach to statistical inference, namely fiducial inference, that also considers Interval estimation.
Estimator	In statistics, an Estimator or point estimate is a statistic (that is, a measurable function of the data) that is used to infer the value of an unknown parameter in a statistical model. The parameter being estimated is sometimes called the estimand. It can be either finite-dimensional , or infinite-dimensional (semi-nonparametric and non-parametric models).
Prediction interval	In statistical inference, specifically predictive inference, a Prediction interval is an estimate of an interval in which future observations will fall, with a certain probability, given what has already been observed. Prediction intervals are often used in regression analysis. Prediction intervals are used in both frequentist statistics and Bayesian statistics: a Prediction interval bears the same relationship to a future observation that a frequentist confidence interval or Bayesian credible interval bears to an unobservable population parameter: Prediction intervals predict the distribution of individual future points, whereas confidence intervals and credible intervals of parameters predict the distribution of estimates of the true population mean or other quantity of interest that cannot be observed.
Sample	In statistics, a Sample is a subset of a population. Typically, the population is very large, making a census or a complete enumeration of all the values in the population impractical or impossible. The Sample represents a subset of manageable size.

Chapter 12. Simple Regression Analysis and Correlation

Chapter 12. Simple Regression Analysis and Correlation

Trend line

A Trend line represents a trend, the long-term movement in time series data after other components have been accounted for. It tells whether a particular data set (say GDP, oil prices or stock prices) have increased or decreased over the period of time. A Trend line could simply be drawn by eye through a set of data points, but more properly their position and slope is calculated using statistical techniques like linear regression. Trend lines typically are straight lines, although some variations use higher degree polynomials depending on the degree of curvature desired in the line.

Forecasting

Forecasting is the process of making statements about events whose actual outcomes (typically) have not yet been observed. A commonplace example might be estimation of the expected value for some variable of interest at some specified future date. Prediction is a similar, but more general term.

Raw data

Raw data is a term for data collected on source which has not been subjected to processing or any other manipulation, it is also known as primary data. It is a relative term. Raw data can be input to a computer program or used in manual analysis procedures such as gathering statistics from a survey.

Chapter 12. Simple Regression Analysis and Correlation

Chapter 13. Multiple Regression Analysis

Regression analysis	In statistics, Regression analysis includes any techniques for modeling and analyzing several variables, when the focus is on the relationship between a dependent variable and one or more independent variables. More specifically, Regression analysis helps us understand how the typical value of the dependent variable changes when any one of the independent variables is varied, while the other independent variables are held fixed. Most commonly, Regression analysis estimates the conditional expectation of the dependent variable given the independent variables -- that is, the average value of the dependent variable when the independent variables are held fixed.
Dependent variable	The terms `dependent variable` and `independent variable` are used in similar but subtly different ways in mathematics and statistics as part of the standard terminology in those subjects. They are used to distinguish between two types of quantities being considered, separating them into those available at the start of a process and those being created by it, where the latter (dependent variables) are dependent on the former (independent variables). The independent variable is typically the variable representing the value being manipulated or changed and the dependent variable is the observed result of the independent variable being manipulated.
Independent variable	The terms `dependent variable` and `Independent variable` are used in similar but subtly different ways in mathematics and statistics as part of the standard terminology in those subjects. They are used to distinguish between two types of quantities being considered, separating them into those available at the start of a process and those being created by it, where the latter (dependent variables) are dependent on the former (Independent variables). The Independent variable is typically the variable being manipulated or changed and the dependent variable is the observed result of the Independent variable being manipulated.
Regression coefficient	The regression coefficient is the slope of the straight line that most closely relates two correlated variables.
Least squares	The method of Least squares is a standard approach to the approximate solution of overdetermined systems, i.e. sets of equations in which there are more equations than unknowns. `Least squares` means that the overall solution minimizes the sum of the squares of the errors made in solving every single equation. The most important application is in data fitting. The best fit in the Least squares sense minimizes the sum of squared residuals, a residual being the difference between an observed value and the fitted value provided by a model.

Chapter 13. Multiple Regression Analysis

Chapter 13. Multiple Regression Analysis

Mann-Whitney U test	In statistics, the Mann-Whitney U test is a non-parametric test for assessing whether two independent samples of observations come from the same distribution. It is one of the best-known non-parametric significance tests. It was proposed initially by Frank Wilcoxon in 1945, for equal sample sizes, and extended to arbitrary sample sizes and in other ways by H. B. Mann and Whitney (1947).
Random sampling	In random sampling every combination of items from the frame, or stratum, has a known probability of occurring, but these probabilities are not necessarily equal. With any form of sampling there is a risk that the sample may not adequately represent the population but with random sampling there is a large body of statistical theory which quantifies the risk and thus enables an appropriate sample size to be chosen.
Systematic sample	A systematic sample is a statistical method involving the selection of a specific interval element from a sampling frame. Using this procedure each element in the population has a known and equal probability of selection. This makes it functionally similar to simple random sampling.
Degrees of freedom	In statistics, the number of degrees of freedom is the number of values in the final calculation of a statistic that are free to vary.
	Estimates of statistical parameters can be based upon different amounts of information or data. The number of independent pieces of information that go into the estimate of a parameter is called the degrees of freedom.
Poisson distribution	In probability theory and statistics, the Poisson distribution is a discrete probability distribution that expresses the probability of a number of events occurring in a fixed period of time if these events occur with a known average rate and independently of the time since the last event.
	The distribution was first introduced by Siméon-Denis Poisson (1781-1840) and published, together with his probability theory, in 1838 in his work Recherches sur la probabilité des jugements en matière criminelle et en matière civile . The work focused on certain random variables N that count, among other things, the number of discrete occurrences (sometimes called `arrivals`) that take place during a time-interval of given length.
Outlier	In statistics, an Outlier is an observation that is numerically distant from the rest of the data. Grubbs defined an Outlier as:

Chapter 13. Multiple Regression Analysis

Chapter 13. Multiple Regression Analysis

	An outlying observation, or Outlier, is one that appears to deviate markedly from other members of the sample in which it occurs.
	Outliers can occur by chance in any distribution, but they are often indicative either of measurement error or that the population has a heavy-tailed distribution.
Residual	Error is a misnomer; an error is the amount by which an observation differs from its expected value; the latter being based on the whole population from which the statistical unit was chosen randomly. A residual, on the other hand, is an observable estimate of the unobservable error.
Scatter plot	A Scatter plot or scattergraph is a type of mathematical diagram using Cartesian coordinates to display values for two variables for a set of data.
	The data is displayed as a collection of points, each having the value of one variable determining the position on the horizontal axis and the value of the other variable determining the position on the vertical axis. This kind of plot is also called a scatter chart, scatter diagram and scatter graph.
Standard error	The Standard error of a method of measurement or estimation is the standard deviation of the sampling distribution associated with the estimation method. The term may also be used to refer to an estimate of that standard deviation, derived from a particular sample used to compute the estimate.
	For example, the sample mean is the usual estimator of a population mean. However, different samples drawn from that same population would in general have different values of the sample mean. The Standard error of the mean is the standard deviation of those sample means over all possible samples (of a given size) drawn from the population. Secondly, the Standard error of the mean can refer to an estimate of that standard deviation, computed from the sample of data being analysed at the time.
Sum of squares	Sum of squares is a concept that permeates much of inferential statistics and descriptive statistics. More properly, it is the sum of squared deviations. Mathematically, it is an unscaled, or unadjusted measure of dispersion (also called variability). When scaled for the number of degrees of freedom, it estimates the variance, or spread of the observations about their mean value.

Chapter 13. Multiple Regression Analysis

Chapter 13. Multiple Regression Analysis

The distance from any point in a collection of data, to the mean of the data, is the deviation. This can be written as $X_i - \overline{X}$, where X_i is the ith data point, and $\overline{X}$ is the estimate of the mean. If all such deviations are squared, then summed, as in $\sum_{i=1}^{n}(X_i - \overline{X})^2$, we have the `Sum of squares` for these data.

ANOVA

In statistics, ANOVA is a collection of statistical models, and their associated procedures, in which the observed variance is partitioned into components due to different sources of variation. In its simplest form ANOVA provides a statistical test of whether or not the means of several groups are all equal, and therefore generalizes Student's two-sample t-test to more than two groups. ANOVAs are helpful because they possess a certain advantage over a two-sample t-test. Doing multiple two-sample t-tests would result in a largely increased chance of committing a type I error. For this reason, ANOVAs are useful in comparing three or more means.

There are three conceptual classes of such models:

· Fixed-effects models assume that the data came from normal populations which may differ only in their means. (Model 1)

· Random effects models assume that the data describe a hierarchy of different populations whose differences are constrained by the hierarchy. (Model 2)

· Mixed-effect models describe the situations where both fixed and random effects are present. (Model 3)

Chapter 13. Multiple Regression Analysis

Chapter 14. Building Multiple Regression Models

Regression analysis	In statistics, Regression analysis includes any techniques for modeling and analyzing several variables, when the focus is on the relationship between a dependent variable and one or more independent variables. More specifically, Regression analysis helps us understand how the typical value of the dependent variable changes when any one of the independent variables is varied, while the other independent variables are held fixed. Most commonly, Regression analysis estimates the conditional expectation of the dependent variable given the independent variables -- that is, the average value of the dependent variable when the independent variables are held fixed.
Linear regression	In statistics, Linear regression is any approach to modeling the relationship between a scalar variable y and one or more variables denoted X. In Linear regression, models of the unknown parameters are estimated from the data using linear functions. Such models are called `linear models.` Most commonly, Linear regression refers to a model in which the conditional mean of y given the value of X is an affine function of X. Less commonly, Linear regression could refer to a model in which the median, or some other quantile of the conditional distribution of y given X is expressed as a linear function of X. Like all forms of regression analysis, Linear regression focuses on the conditional probability distribution of y given X, rather than on the joint probability distribution of y and X, which is the domain of multivariate analysis.
	Linear regression was the first type of regression analysis to be studied rigorously, and to be used extensively in practical applications.
Nonlinear regression	In statistics, Nonlinear regression is a form of regression analysis in which observational data are modeled by a function which is a nonlinear combination of the model parameters and depends on one or more independent variables. The data are fitted by a method of successive approximations.
	The data consist of error-free independent variables (explanatory variable), x, and their associated observed dependent variables (response variable), y. Each y is modeled as a random variable with a mean given by a nonlinear function $f(x,\beta)$. Systematic error may be present but its treatment is outside the scope of regression analysis. If the independent variables are not error-free, this is an errors-in-variables model, also outside this scope.
	For example, the Michaelis-Menten model for enzyme kinetics

Chapter 14. Building Multiple Regression Models

Chapter 14. Building Multiple Regression Models

$$v = \frac{V_{max}[S]}{K_m + [S]}$$

can be written as

$$f(x, \boldsymbol{\beta}) = \frac{\beta_1 x}{\beta_2 + x}$$

where β_1 is the parameter V_{max}, β_2 is the parameter K_m and $[S]$ is the independent variable, x. This function is nonlinear because it cannot be expressed as a linear combination of the βs.

Polynomial regression

In statistics, Polynomial regression is a form of linear regression in which the relationship between the independent variable x and the dependent variable y is modeled as an nth order polynomial. Polynomial regression fits a nonlinear relationship between the value of x and the corresponding conditional mean of y, denoted E, and has been used to describe nonlinear phenomena such as the growth rate of tissues, the distribution of carbon isotopes in lake sediments , and the progression of disease epidemics. Although Polynomial regression fits a nonlinear model to the data, as a statistical estimation problem it is linear, in the sense that the regression function E is linear in the unknown parameters that are estimated from the data.

Polynomial regression models are usually fit using the method of least squares. The least-squares method minimizes the variance of the unbiased estimators of the coefficients, under the conditions of the Gauss-Markov theorem. The least-squares method was published in 1805 by Legendre and in 1809 by Gauss. The first design of an experiment for Polynomial regression appeared in an 1815 paper of Gergonne. In the twentieth century, Polynomial regression played an important role in the development of regression analysis, with a greater emphasis on issues of design and inference. More recently, the use of polynomial models has been complemented by other methods, with non-polynomial models having advantages for some classes of problems. The goal of regression analysis is to model the expected value of a dependent variable y in terms of the value of an independent variable (or vector of independent variables) x. In simple linear regression, the model

$$y = a_0 + a_1 x + \varepsilon,$$

Chapter 14. Building Multiple Regression Models

Chapter 14. Building Multiple Regression Models

	is used, where ε is an unobserved random error with mean zero conditicned on a scalar variable x. In this model, for each unit increase in the value of x, the conditional expectation of y increases by a_1 units.
Coefficient of determination	In statistics, the Coefficient of determination, R^2 is used in the context of statistical models whose main purpose is the prediction of future outcomes on the basis of other related information. It is the proportion of variability in a data set that is accounted for by the statistical model. It provides a measure of how well future outcomes are likely to be predicted by the model.
	There are several different definitions of R^2 which are only sometimes equivalent. One class of such cases includes that of linear regression. In this case, R^2 is simply the square of the sample correlation coefficient between the outcomes and their predicted values, or in the case of simple linear regression, between the outcome and the values being used for prediction. In such cases, the values vary from 0 to 1. Important cases where the computational definition of R^2 can yield negative values, depending on the definition used, arise where the predictions which are being compared to the corresponding outcome have not derived from a model-fitting procedure using those data.
Regression coefficient	The regression coefficient is the slope of the straight line that most closely relates two correlated variables.
Poisson distribution	In probability theory and statistics, the Poisson distribution is a discrete probability distribution that expresses the probability of a number of events occurring in a fixed period of time if these events occur with a known average rate and independently of the time since the last event.
	The distribution was first introduced by Siméon-Denis Poisson (1781-1840) and published, together with his probability theory, in 1838 in his work Recherches sur la probabilité des jugements en matière criminelle et en matière civile . The work focused on certain random variables N that count, among other things, the number of discrete occurrences (sometimes called `arrivals`) that take place during a time-interval of given length.
Interaction	Interaction is a kind of action that occurs as two or more objects have an effect upon one another. The idea of a two-way effect is essential in the concept of Interaction, as opposed to a one-way causal effect. A closely related term is interconnectivity, which deals with the Interactions of Interactions within systems: combinations of many simple Interactions can lead to surprising emergent phenomena.

Chapter 14. Building Multiple Regression Models

Chapter 14. Building Multiple Regression Models

Mann-Whitney U test	In statistics, the Mann-Whitney U test is a non-parametric test for assessing whether two independent samples of observations come from the same distribution. It is one of the best-known non-parametric significance tests. It was proposed initially by Frank Wilcoxon in 1945, for equal sample sizes, and extended to arbitrary sample sizes and in other ways by H. B. Mann and Whitney (1947).
Dummy variable	In regression analysis, a Dummy variable is one that takes the values 0 or 1 to indicate the absence or presence of some categorical effect that may be expected to shift the outcome. For example, in econometric time series analysis, Dummy variables may be used to indicate the occurrence of wars, or major strikes. It could thus be thought of as a truth value represented as a numerical value 0 or 1.
Friedman test	The Friedman test is a non-parametric statistical test developed by the U.S. economist Milton Friedman. Similar to the parametric repeated measures ANOVA, it is used to detect differences in treatments across multiple test attempts. The procedure involves ranking each row (or block) together, then considering the values of ranks by columns. Applicable to complete block designs, it is thus a special case of the Durbin test.

Classic examples of use are:

· n wine judges rate k different wines. Are any wines ranked consistently higher or lower than the others?

· n wines are rated by k different judges. Are the judges ratings consistent with each other?

· n welders use k welding torches, and the ensuing welds were rated on quality. Do any of the torches produce consistently better or worse welds? |
| Stepwise regression | In statistics, Stepwise regression includes regression models in which the choice of predictive variables is carried out by an automatic procedure. Usually, this takes the form of a sequence of F-tests, but other techniques are possible, such as t-tests, adjusted R-square, Akaike information criterion, Bayesian information criterion, Mallows` Cp, or false discovery rate. |

Chapter 14. Building Multiple Regression Models

Chapter 14. Building Multiple Regression Models

The main approaches are:

· Forward selection, which involves starting with no variables in the model, trying out the variables one by one and including them if they are `statistically significant`

· Backward elimination, which involves starting with all candidate variables and testing them one by one for statistical significance, deleting any that are not significant

· Methods that are a combination of the above, testing at each stage for variables to be included or excluded

A widely used algorithm was first proposed by Efroymson (1960). This is an automatic procedure for statistical model selection in cases where there are a large number of potential explanatory variables, and no underlying theory on which to base the model selection.

Backward elimination	In Stepwise regression backward elimination involves starting with all candidate variables and testing them one by one for statistical significance, deleting any that are not significant.
Forward selection	In stepwise regression Forward selection involves starting with no variables in the model, trying out the variables one by one and including them if they are `statistically significant`. Usually, this takes the form of a sequence of F-tests, but other techniques are possible, such as t-tests, adjusted R-square, Akaike information criterion, Bayesian information criterion, Mallows' Cp, or false discovery rate.
Multicollinearity	Multicollinearity is a statistical phenomenon in which two or more predictor variables in a multiple regression model are highly correlated. In this situation the coefficient estimates may change erratically in response to small changes in the model or the data. Multicollinearity does not reduce the predictive power or reliability of the model as a whole; it only affects calculations regarding individual predictors. Collinearity is a linear relationship between two explanatory variables. Two variables are collinear if there is an exact linear relationship between the two. For example, X_1 and X_2 are collinear if $$X_1 = \lambda X_2$$

Chapter 14. Building Multiple Regression Models

Chapter 14. Building Multiple Regression Models

Multicollinearity refers to a situation in which two or more explanatory variables in a multiple regression model are highly correlated. We have perfect Multicollinearity if the correlation between two independent variables is equal to 1 or -1. In practice, we rarely face perfect Multicollinearity in a data set. More commonly, the issue of Multicollinearity arises when there is a high degree of correlation between two or more independent variables.

Variance

In probability theory and statistics, the Variance is used as one of several descriptors of a distribution. It describes how far values lie from the mean. In particular, the Variance is one of the moments of a distribution.

Variance inflation factor

In statistics, the Variance inflation factor is a method of detecting the severity of multicollinearity. More precisely, the Variance inflation factor is an index which measures how much the variance of a coefficient (square of the standard deviation) is increased because of collinearity.
Consider the following regression equation with k independent variables:

$$Y = \beta_0 + \beta_1 X_1 + \beta_2 X_2 + \dots + \beta_k X_k + \varepsilon$$

VIF can be calculated in three steps:

Step one
Calculate k different Variance inflation factors, one for each X_i by first running an ordinary least square regression that has X_i as a function of all the other explanatory variables in the first equation.

If i = 1, for example, the equation would be

$$X_1 = \alpha_2 X_2 + \alpha_3 X_3 + \dots + \alpha_k X_k + c_0 + e$$

where c_0 is a constant and e is the error term.

Step two

Chapter 14. Building Multiple Regression Models

Chapter 14. Building Multiple Regression Models

Then, calculate the Variance inflation factor factor for $\hat{\beta}_i$ with the following formula:

$$\mathrm{VIF}(\hat{\beta}_i) = \frac{1}{1 - R_i^2}$$

where R_i^2 is the coefficient of determination of the regression equation in step one.

Step three

Analyze the magnitude of multicollinearity by considering the size of the $VIF(\hat{\beta}_i)$. A common rule of thumb is that if $VIF(\hat{\beta}_i) > 5$ then multicollinearity is high. Also 10 has been proposed as a cut off value.

ANOVA

In statistics, ANOVA is a collection of statistical models, and their associated procedures, in which the observed variance is partitioned into components due to different sources of variation. In its simplest form ANOVA provides a statistical test of whether or not the means of several groups are all equal, and therefore generalizes Student's two-sample t-test to more than two groups. ANOVAs are helpful because they possess a certain advantage over a two-sample t-test. Doing multiple two-sample t-tests would result in a largely increased chance of committing a type I error. For this reason, ANOVAs are useful in comparing three or more means.
There are three conceptual classes of such models:

· Fixed-effects models assume that the data came from normal populations which may differ only in their means. (Model 1)

· Random effects models assume that the data describe a hierarchy of different populations whose differences are constrained by the hierarchy. (Model 2)

· Mixed-effect models describe the situations where both fixed and random effects are present. (Model 3)

Independent variable

The terms `dependent variable` and `Independent variable` are used in similar but subtly different ways in mathematics and statistics as part of the standard terminology in those subjects. They are used to distinguish between two types of quantities being considered, separating them into those available at the start of a process and those being created by it, where the latter (dependent variables) are dependent on the former (Independent variables).

Chapter 14. Building Multiple Regression Models

Chapter 14. Building Multiple Regression Models

The Independent variable is typically the variable being manipulated or changed and the dependent variable is the observed result of the Independent variable being manipulated.

Chapter 14. Building Multiple Regression Models

Chapter 15. Time-Series Forecasting and Index Numbers

Forecasting

Forecasting is the process of making statements about events whose actual outcomes (typically) have not yet been observed. A commonplace example might be estimation of the expected value for some variable of interest at some specified future date. Prediction is a similar, but more general term.

Mean

In statistics, mean has two related meanings:

· the arithmetic mean .

· the expected value of a random variable, which is also called the population mean.
It is sometimes stated that the `mean` means average. This is incorrect if `mean` is taken in the specific sense of `arithmetic mean` as there are different types of averages: the mean, median, and mode.

Absolute deviation

In statistics, the Absolute deviation of an element of a data set is the absolute difference between that element and a given point. Typically the point from which the deviation is measured is a measure of central tendency, most often the median or sometimes the mean of the data set.

$$D_i = : x_i - m(X) :$$

where

D_i is the Absolute deviation,
x_i is the data element
and $m(X)$ is the chosen measure of central tendency of the data set--sometimes the mean , but most often the median.

Forecast Error

In statistics, a Forecast error is the difference between the actual or real and the predicted or forecast value of a time series or any other phenomenon of interest.

In simple cases, a forecast is compared with an outcome at a single time-point and a summary of Forecast errors is constructed over a collection of such time-points. Here the forecast may be assessed using the difference or using a proportional error.

Chapter 15. Time-Series Forecasting and Index Numbers

Chapter 15. Time-Series Forecasting and Index Numbers

Mean square error

In statistics, the Mean square error of an estimator is one of many ways to quantify the difference between an estimator and the true value of the quantity being estimated. Mean square error is a risk function, corresponding to the expected value of the squared error loss or quadratic loss. Mean square error measures the average of the square of the `error.` The error is the amount by which the estimator differs from the quantity to be estimated.

Smoothing

In statistics and image processing, to smooth a data set is to create an approximating function that attempts to capture important patterns in the data, while leaving out noise or other fine-scale structures/rapid phenomena. Many different algorithms are used in Smoothing. One of the most common algorithms is the `moving average`, often used to try to capture important trends in repeated statistical surveys.

Moving average

In statistics, a Moving average is a type of finite impulse response filter used to analyze a set of data points by creating a series of averages of different subsets of the full data set.

Given a series of numbers and a fixed subset size, the Moving average can be obtained by first taking the average of the first subset. The fixed subset size is then shifted forward, creating a new subset of numbers, which is averaged.
A simple Moving average is the unweighted mean of the previous n data points. For example, a 10-day simple Moving average of closing price is the mean of the previous 10 days` closing prices. If those prices are $p_M, p_{M-1}, \cdots, p_{M-9}$ then the formula is

$$SMA = \frac{p_M + p_{M-1} + \cdots + p_{M-9}}{10}$$

When calculating successive values, a new value comes into the sum and an old value drops out, meaning a full summation each time is unnecessary,

$$SMA_{\text{today}} = SMA_{\text{yesterday}} - \frac{p_{M-n}}{n} + \frac{p_M}{n}$$

Exponential smoothing

Exponential smoothing is a technique that can be applied to time series data, either to produce smoothed data for presentation, or to make forecasts. The time series data themselves are a sequence of observations. The observed phenomenon may be an essentially random process, or it may be an orderly, but noisy, process.

Chapter 15. Time-Series Forecasting and Index Numbers

Chapter 15. Time-Series Forecasting and Index Numbers

Poisson distribution	In probability theory and statistics, the Poisson distribution is a discrete probability distribution that expresses the probability of a number of events occurring in a fixed period of time if these events occur with a known average rate and independently of the time since the last event. The distribution was first introduced by Siméon-Denis Poisson (1781-1840) and published, together with his probability theory, in 1838 in his work Recherches sur la probabilité des jugements en matière criminelle et en matière civile . The work focused on certain random variables N that count, among other things, the number of discrete occurrences (sometimes called `arrivals`) that take place during a time-interval of given length.
Linear regression	In statistics, Linear regression is any approach to modeling the relationship between a scalar variable y and one or more variables denoted X. In Linear regression, models of the unknown parameters are estimated from the data using linear functions. Such models are called `linear models.` Most commonly, Linear regression refers to a model in which the conditional mean of y given the value of X is an affine function of X. Less commonly, Linear regression could refer to a model in which the median, or some other quantile of the conditional distribution of y given X is expressed as a linear function of X. Like all forms of regression analysis, Linear regression focuses on the conditional probability distribution of y given X, rather than on the joint probability distribution of y and X, which is the domain of multivariate analysis. Linear regression was the first type of regression analysis to be studied rigorously, and to be used extensively in practical applications.
Trend analysis	The term `Trend analysis` refers to the concept of collecting information and attempting to spot a pattern, or trend, in the information. In some fields of study, the term `Trend analysis` has more formally-defined meanings. In project management Trend analysis is a mathematical technique that uses historical results to predict future outcome.
Coefficient of determination	In statistics, the Coefficient of determination, R^2 is used in the context of statistical models whose main purpose is the prediction of future outcomes on the basis of other related information. It is the proportion of variability in a data set that is accounted for by the statistical model. It provides a measure of how well future outcomes are likely to be predicted by the model.

Chapter 15. Time-Series Forecasting and Index Numbers

Chapter 15. Time-Series Forecasting and Index Numbers

There are several different definitions of R^2 which are only sometimes equivalent. One class of such cases includes that of linear regression. In this case, R^2 is simply the square of the sample correlation coefficient between the outcomes and their predicted values, or in the case of simple linear regression, between the outcome and the values being used for prediction. In such cases, the values vary from 0 to 1. Important cases where the computational definition of R^2 can yield negative values, depending on the definition used, arise where the predictions which are being compared to the corresponding outcome have not derived from a model-fitting procedure using those data.

Regression coefficient	The regression coefficient is the slope of the straight line that most closely relates two correlated variables.
Correlation	In statistics, Correlation indicates the strength and direction of a relationship between two random variables. The commonest use refers to a linear relationship, but the concept of nonlinear Correlation is also used. In general statistical usage, Correlation or co-relation refers to the departure of two random variables from independence.
Rank correlation	In statistics, Rank correlation is the study of relationships between different rankings on the same set of items. A Rank correlation coefficient measures the correspondence between two rankings and assesses its significance. Two of the more popular Rank correlation statistics are · Spearman's Rank correlation coefficient (Spearman's ρ) · Kendall's tau Rank correlation coefficient (Kendall's τ) An increasing Rank correlation coefficient implies increasing agreement between rankings. The coefficient is inside the interval [−1, 1] and assumes the value: · −1 if the disagreement between the two rankings is perfect; one ranking is the reverse of the other. · 0 if the rankings are completely independent. · 1 if the agreement between the two rankings is perfect; the two rankings are the same.

Chapter 15. Time-Series Forecasting and Index Numbers

Chapter 15. Time-Series Forecasting and Index Numbers

	Following the Diaconis reference below, a ranking can be seen as a permutation of a set of objects.
Index number	An Index number is an economic data figure reflecting price or quantity compared with a standard or base value. The base usually equals 100 and the Index number is usually expressed as 100 times the ratio to the base value. For example, if a commodity costs twice as much in 1970 as it did in 1960, its Index number would be 200 relative to 1960. Index numbers are used especially to compare business activity, the cost of living, and employment.
ANOVA	In statistics, ANOVA is a collection of statistical models, and their associated procedures, in which the observed variance is partitioned into components due to different sources of variation. In its simplest form ANOVA provides a statistical test of whether or not the means of several groups are all equal, and therefore generalizes Student`s two-sample t-test to more than two groups. ANOVAs are helpful because they possess a certain advantage over a two-sample t-test. Doing multiple two-sample t-tests would result in a largely increased chance of committing a type I error. For this reason, ANOVAs are useful in comparing three or more means. There are three conceptual classes of such models: · Fixed-effects models assume that the data came from normal populations which may differ only in their means. (Model 1) · Random effects models assume that the data describe a hierarchy of different populations whose differences are constrained by the hierarchy. (Model 2) · Mixed-effect models describe the situations where both fixed and random effects are present. (Model 3)
Autocorrelation	Autocorrelation is the cross-correlation of a signal with itself. Informally, it is the similarity between observations as a function of the time separation between them. It is a mathematical tool for finding repeating patterns, such as the presence of a periodic signal which has been buried under noise, or identifying the missing fundamental frequency in a signal implied by its harmonic frequencies.

Chapter 15. Time-Series Forecasting and Index Numbers

Chapter 15. Time-Series Forecasting and Index Numbers

Regression analysis	In statistics, Regression analysis includes any techniques for modeling and analyzing several variables, when the focus is on the relationship between a dependent variable and one or more independent variables. More specifically, Regression analysis helps us understand how the typical value of the dependent variable changes when any one of the independent variables is varied, while the other independent variables are held fixed. Most commonly, Regression analysis estimates the conditional expectation of the dependent variable given the independent variables -- that is, the average value of the dependent variable when the independent variables are held fixed.
Independent variable	The terms `dependent variable` and `Independent variable` are used in similar but subtly different ways in mathematics and statistics as part of the standard terminology in those subjects. They are used to distinguish between two types of quantities being considered, separating them into those available at the start of a process and those being created by it, where the latter (dependent variables) are dependent on the former (Independent variables). The Independent variable is typically the variable being manipulated or changed and the dependent variable is the observed result of the Independent variable being manipulated.
Dummy variable	In regression analysis, a Dummy variable is one that takes the values 0 or 1 to indicate the absence or presence of some categorical effect that may be expected to shift the outcome. For example, in econometric time series analysis, Dummy variables may be used to indicate the occurrence of wars, or major strikes. It could thus be thought of as a truth value represented as a numerical value 0 or 1.
Probability sampling	Probability sampling is technique of sampling that uses som form of random selection. In order to have randon selection, there must be a set up process that assuraes that the different units in the population have equal probabilities of being chosen.
Statistical dispersion	In statistics, Statistical dispersion is variability or spread in a variable or a probability distribution. Common examples of measures of Statistical dispersion are the variance, standard deviation and interquartile range. Dispersion is contrasted with location or central tendency, and together they are the most used properties of distributions.

Chapter 15. Time-Series Forecasting and Index Numbers

Chapter 15. Time-Series Forecasting and Index Numbers

Friedman test	The Friedman test is a non-parametric statistical test developed by the U.S. economist Milton Friedman. Similar to the parametric repeated measures ANOVA, it is used to detect differences in treatments across multiple test attempts. The procedure involves ranking each row (or block) together, then considering the values of ranks by columns. Applicable to complete block designs, it is thus a special case of the Durbin test.

Classic examples of use are:

· n wine judges rate k different wines. Are any wines ranked consistently higher or lower than the others?

· n wines are rated by k different judges. Are the judges ratings consistent with each other?

· n welders use k welding torches, and the ensuing welds were rated on quality. Do any of the torches produce consistently better or worse welds?

Chapter 15. Time-Series Forecasting and Index Numbers

Chapter 16. Analysis of Categorical Data

Categorical data

In statistics, Categorical data is that part of an observed dataset that consists of categorical variables, or for data that has been converted into that form, for example as grouped data. More specifically, Categorical data may derive from either or both of observations made of qualitative data, where the observations are summarised as counts or cross tabulations, or of quantitative data, where observations might be directly observed counts of events happening or they might counts of values that occur within given intervals. Often, purely Categorical data are summarised in the form of a contingency table.

Data analysis

Analysis of data is a process of inspecting, cleaning, transforming, and modeling data with the goal of highlighting useful information, suggesting conclusions, and supporting decision making. Data analysis has multiple facets and approaches, encompassing diverse techniques under a variety of names, in different business, science, and social science domains.

Data mining is a particular Data analysis technique that focuses on modeling and knowledge discovery for predictive rather than purely descriptive purposes.

Chi-square distribution

In probability theory and statistics, the Chi-square distribution with k degrees of freedom is the distribution of a sum of the squares of k independent standard normal random variables. It is one of the most widely used probability distributions in inferential statistics, e.g. in hypothesis testing, or in construction of confidence intervals.

The best-known situations in which the Chi-square distribution is used are the common chi-square tests for goodness of fit of an observed distribution to a theoretical one, and of the independence of two criteria of classification of qualitative data. Many other statistical tests also lead to a use of this distribution, like Friedman`s analysis of variance by ranks.
If X_1, â€¦, X_k are independent, standard normal random variables, then the sum of their squares

$$Q = \sum_{i=1}^{k} X_i^2$$

is distributed according to the Chi-square distribution with k degrees of freedom. This is usually denoted as

Chapter 16. Analysis of Categorical Data

Chapter 16. Analysis of Categorical Data

$$Q \sim \chi^2(k) \text{ or } Q \sim \chi_k^2$$

The Chi-square distribution has one parameter: k -- a positive integer that specifies the number of degrees of freedom (i.e. the number of X_i's)

ANOVA

In statistics, ANOVA is a collection of statistical models, and their associated procedures, in which the observed variance is partitioned into components due to different sources of variation. In its simplest form ANOVA provides a statistical test of whether or not the means of several groups are all equal, and therefore generalizes Student's two-sample t-test to more than two groups. ANOVAs are helpful because they possess a certain advantage over a two-sample t-test. Doing multiple two-sample t-tests would result in a largely increased chance of committing a type I error. For this reason, ANOVAs are useful in comparing three or more means.
There are three conceptual classes of such models:

· Fixed-effects models assume that the data came from normal populations which may differ only in their means. (Model 1)

· Random effects models assume that the data describe a hierarchy of different populations whose differences are constrained by the hierarchy. (Model 2)

· Mixed-effect models describe the situations where both fixed and random effects are present. (Model 3)

Chi-square test

`Chi-square test` also known as Pearson's Chi-square test.

A Chi-square test is any statistical hypothesis test in which the sampling distribution of the test statistic is a chi-square distribution when the null hypothesis is true, or any in which this is asymptotically true, meaning that the sampling distribution (if the null hypothesis is true) can be made to approximate a chi-square distribution as closely as desired by making the sample size large enough.

Some examples of chi-squared tests where the chi-square distribution is only approximately valid:

Chapter 16. Analysis of Categorical Data

Chapter 16. Analysis of Categorical Data

· Pearson`s Chi-square test, also known as the chi-square goodness-of-fit test or Chi-square test for independence. When mentioned without any modifiers or without other precluding context, this test is usually understood .

· Yates` Chi-square test, also known as Yates` correction for continuity.

· Mantel-Haenszel Chi-square test.

· Linear-by-linear association Chi-square test.

· The portmanteau test in time-series analysis, testing for the presence of autocorrelation

· Likelihood-ratio tests in general statistical modelling, for testing whether there is evidence of the need to move from a simple model to a more complicated one (where the simple model is nested within the complicated one).

Contingency table

In statistics, a Contingency table is often used to record and analyze the relation between two or more categorical variables. It displays the (multivariate) frequency distribution of the variables in a matrix format.

The term Contingency table was first used by Karl Pearson in `On the Theory of Contingency and Its Relation to Association and Normal Correlation`, part of the Drapers` Company Research Memoirs Biometric Series I published in 1904.

Null hypothesis

The practice of science involves formulating and testing hypotheses, assertions that are falsifiable using a test of observed data. The Null hypothesis typically proposes a general or default position, such as that there is no relationship between two measured phenomena, or that a potential treatment has no effect. The term was originally coined by English geneticist and statistician Ronald Fisher. It is typically paired with a second hypothesis, the alternative hypothesis, which asserts a particular relationship between the phenomena. Jerzy Neyman and Egon Pearson formalized the notion of the alternative. The alternative need not be the logical negation of the Null hypothesis and is the predicted hypothesis you would get from the experiment. The use of alternative hypotheses was not part of Fisher`s formulation, but became standard.

Chapter 16. Analysis of Categorical Data

Chapter 17. Nonparametric Statistics

Parametric statistics

Parametric statistics is a branch of statistics that assumes data come from a type of probability distribution and makes inferences about the parameters of the distribution. Most well-known elementary statistical methods are parametric.

Generally speaking parametric methods make more assumptions than non-parametric methods. If those extra assumptions are correct, parametric methods can produce more accurate and precise estimates. They are said to have more statistical power. However, if those assumptions are incorrect, parametric methods can be very misleading. For that reason they are often not considered robust. On the other hand, parametric formulae are often simpler to write down and faster to compute. In some, but definitely not all cases, their simplicity makes up for their non-robustness, especially if care is taken to examine diagnostic statistics.

Mann-Whitney U test

In statistics, the Mann-Whitney U test is a non-parametric test for assessing whether two independent samples of observations come from the same distribution. It is one of the best-known non-parametric significance tests. It was proposed initially by Frank Wilcoxon in 1945, for equal sample sizes, and extended to arbitrary sample sizes and in other ways by H. B. Mann and Whitney (1947).

Runs test

The Runs test is a non-parametric test that checks a randomness hypothesis for a two-valued data sequence. More precisely, it can be used to test the hypothesis that the elements of the sequence are mutually independent.

A `run` of a sequence is a maximal non-empty segment of the sequence consisting of adjacent equal elements. For example, the sequence `++++---+++--++++++----` consists of six runs, three of which consist of +'s and the others of –'s. If +s and –s alternate randomly, the number of runs in a sequence of length N for which it is given that there are N_+ occurrences of + and N_- occurrences of - (so $N = N_+ + N_-$) is a random variable whose conditional distribution - given the observation of N_+ and N_- - is approximately normal with:

· mean

$$\mu = \frac{2\,N_+\,N_-}{N} + 1,$$

· variance

$$\sigma^2 = \frac{2\,N_+\,N_-\,(2\,N_+\,N_- - N)}{N^2\,(N-1)} = \frac{(\mu-1)(\mu-2)}{N-1}.$$

Chapter 17. Nonparametric Statistics

Chapter 17. Nonparametric Statistics

Correlation

In statistics, Correlation indicates the strength and direction of a relationship between two random variables. The commonest use refers to a linear relationship, but the concept of nonlinear Correlation is also used. In general statistical usage, Correlation or co-relation refers to the departure of two random variables from independence.

Random sample

A sample is a subject chosen from a population for investigation. A Random sample is one chosen by a method involving an unpredictable component. Random sampling can also refer to taking a number of independent observations from the same probability distribution, without involving any real population.

Rank correlation

In statistics, Rank correlation is the study of relationships between different rankings on the same set of items. A Rank correlation coefficient measures the correspondence between two rankings and assesses its significance.

Two of the more popular Rank correlation statistics are

· Spearman`s Rank correlation coefficient (Spearman`s ρ)

· Kendall`s tau Rank correlation coefficient (Kendall`s τ)
An increasing Rank correlation coefficient implies increasing agreement between rankings. The coefficient is inside the interval $[-1, 1]$ and assumes the value:

· -1 if the disagreement between the two rankings is perfect; one ranking is the reverse of the other.

· 0 if the rankings are completely independent.

· 1 if the agreement between the two rankings is perfect; the two rankings are the same.

Following the Diaconis reference below, a ranking can be seen as a permutation of a set of objects.

Tree diagram

In mathematics and statistical methods, a Tree diagram is used to determine the probability of getting specific results where the possibilities are nested.

Chapter 17. Nonparametric Statistics

Chapter 17. Nonparametric Statistics

Small-sample	Small-sample correction is a correction to the information or the uncertainty measure to account for this effect. In terms of statistics, the uncertainty measure is biased when there are small number of samples.
Poisson distribution	In probability theory and statistics, the Poisson distribution is a discrete probability distribution that expresses the probability of a number of events occurring in a fixed period of time if these events occur with a known average rate and independently of the time since the last event. The distribution was first introduced by Siméon-Denis Poisson (1781-1840) and published, together with his probability theory, in 1838 in his work Recherches sur la probabilité des jugements en matière criminelle et en matière civile . The work focused on certain random variables N that count, among other things, the number of discrete occurrences (sometimes called `arrivals`) that take place during a time-interval of given length.
Score	In statistics, the Score or Score function is the partial derivative, with respect to some parameter θ, of the logarithm (commonly the natural logarithm) of the likelihood function. If the observation is X and its likelihood is L(θ;X), then the Score V can be found through the chain rule: $$V = \frac{\partial}{\partial \theta} \log L(\theta; X) = \frac{1}{L(\theta; X)} \frac{\partial L(\theta; X)}{\partial \theta}.$$ Note that V is a function of θ and the observation X, so that, in general, it is not a statistic. Note also that V indicates the sensitivity of L(θ;X) (its variation normalized by its value.)
Friedman test	The Friedman test is a non-parametric statistical test developed by the U.S. economist Milton Friedman. Similar to the parametric repeated measures ANOVA, it is used to detect differences in treatments across multiple test attempts. The procedure involves ranking each row (or block) together, then considering the values of ranks by columns. Applicable to complete block designs, it is thus a special case of the Durbin test. Classic examples of use are: · n wine judges rate k different wines. Are any wines ranked consistently higher or lower than the others?

Chapter 17. Nonparametric Statistics

Chapter 17. Nonparametric Statistics

· n wines are rated by k different judges. Are the judges ratings consistent with each other?

· n welders use k welding torches, and the ensuing welds were rated on quality. Do any of the torches produce consistently better or worse welds?

ANOVA

In statistics, ANOVA is a collection of statistical models, and their associated procedures, in which the observed variance is partitioned into components due to different sources of variation. In its simplest form ANOVA provides a statistical test of whether or not the means of several groups are all equal, and therefore generalizes Student`s two-sample t-test to more than two groups.
ANOVAs are helpful because they possess a certain advantage over a two-sample t-test. Doing multiple two-sample t-tests would result in a largely increased chance of committing a type I error. For this reason, ANOVAs are useful in comparing three or more means.
There are three conceptual classes of such models:

· Fixed-effects models assume that the data came from normal populations which may differ only in their means. (Model 1)

· Random effects models assume that the data describe a hierarchy of different populations whose differences are constrained by the hierarchy. (Model 2)

· Mixed-effect models describe the situations where both fixed and random effects are present. (Model 3)

Chapter 17. Nonparametric Statistics

Chapter 18. Statistical Quality Control

Failure modes and effects analysis	A Failure modes and effects analysis is a procedure in product development and operations management for analysis of potential failure modes within a system for classification by the severity and likelihood of the failures. A successful failure modes effects analysis activity helps a team to identify potential failure modes based on past experience with similar products or processes, enabling the team to design those failures out of the system with the minimum of effort and resource expenditure, thereby reducing development time and costs. It is widely used in manufacturing industries in various phases of the product life cycle and is now increasingly finding use in the service industry.
Mode	In statistics, the Mode is the value that occurs the most frequently in a data set or a probability distribution. In some fields, notably education, sample data are often called scores, and the sample Mode is known as the modal score. Like the statistical mean and the median, the Mode is a way of capturing important information about a random variable or a population in a single quantity.
Six Sigma	Six sigma is a business management strategy, originally developed by Motorola, that today enjoys widespread application in many sectors of industry. six sigma seeks to identify and remove the causes of defects and errors in manufacturing and business processes. It uses a set of quality management methods, including statistical methods, and creates a special infrastructure of people within the organization (`Black Belts` etc.)
Rectangular distribution	A rectangular distribution is a distribution where all values occur with equal frequency.
Ishikawa diagram	Ishikawa diagrams (also called fishbone diagrams or cause-and-effect diagrams) are diagrams that show the causes of a certain event. Common uses of the Ishikawa diagram are product design and quality defect prevention, to identify potential factors causing an overall effect. Each cause or reason for imperfection is a source of variation.
Flowchart	A Flowchart is a diagrammatic representation of a step-by-step solution to a given problem. It is a common type of diagram, that represents an algorithm or process, showing the steps as boxes of various kinds, and their order by connecting these with arrows. Data is represented in these boxes, and arrows connecting them represent flow / direction of flow of data.
Pareto analysis	Pareto analysis is a statistical technique in decision making that is used for selection of a limited number of tasks that produce significant overall effect. It uses the Pareto principle - the idea that by doing 20% of work, 80% of the advantage of doing the entire job can be generated. Or in terms of quality improvement, a large majority of problems (80%) are produced by a few key causes (20%).

Chapter 18. Statistical Quality Control

Chapter 18. Statistical Quality Control

Pareto chart	A Pareto chart is a type of chart that contains both bars and a line graph, where individual values are represented in descending order by bars, and the cumulative total is represented by the line.
	The left vertical axis is the frequency of occurrence, but it can alternatively represent cost or another important unit of measure. The right vertical axis is the cumulative percentage of the total number of occurrences, total cost, or total of the particular unit of measure.
Control chart	Control charts, also known as Shewhart charts or process-behaviour charts, in statistical process control are tools used to determine whether a manufacturing or business process is in a state of statistical control or not. If the chart indicates that the process is currently under control then it can be used with confidence to predict the future performance of the process. If the chart indicates that the process being monitored is not in control, the pattern it reveals can help determine the source of variation to be eliminated to bring the process back into control.
ANOVA	In statistics, ANOVA is a collection of statistical models, and their associated procedures, in which the observed variance is partitioned into components due to different sources of variation. In its simplest form ANOVA provides a statistical test of whether or not the means of several groups are all equal, and therefore generalizes Student`s two-sample t-test to more than two groups. ANOVAs are helpful because they possess a certain advantage over a two-sample t-test. Doing multiple two-sample t-tests would result in a largely increased chance of committing a type I error. For this reason, ANOVAs are useful in comparing three or more means. There are three conceptual classes of such models: · Fixed-effects models assume that the data came from normal populations which may differ only in their means. (Model 1) · Random effects models assume that the data describe a hierarchy of different populations whose differences are constrained by the hierarchy. (Model 2) · Mixed-effect models describe the situations where both fixed and random effects are present. (Model 3)

Chapter 18. Statistical Quality Control

Chapter 18. Statistical Quality Control

Histogram	A histogram is a graphical display of tabulated frequencies. That is, a histogram is the graphical version of a table which shows what proportion of cases fall into each of several or many specified categories. The categories are usually specified as nonoverlapping intervals of some variable. The categories bars must be adjacent.
Poisson distribution	In probability theory and statistics, the Poisson distribution is a discrete probability distribution that expresses the probability of a number of events occurring in a fixed period of time if these events occur with a known average rate and independently of the time since the last event.
	The distribution was first introduced by Siméon-Denis Poisson (1781-1840) and published, together with his probability theory, in 1838 in his work Recherches sur la probabilité des jugements en matière criminelle et en matière civile . The work focused on certain random variables N that count, among other things, the number of discrete occurrences (sometimes called `arrivals`) that take place during a time-interval of given length.
Exponential smoothing	Exponential smoothing is a technique that can be applied to time series data, either to produce smoothed data for presentation, or to make forecasts. The time series data themselves are a sequence of observations. The observed phenomenon may be an essentially random process, or it may be an orderly, but noisy, process.
Statistical dispersion	In statistics, Statistical dispersion is variability or spread in a variable or a probability distribution. Common examples of measures of Statistical dispersion are the variance, standard deviation and interquartile range.
	Dispersion is contrasted with location or central tendency, and together they are the most used properties of distributions.
Deviation	In mathematics and statistics, deviation is a measure of difference for interval and ratio variables between the observed value and the mean. The sign of deviation, either positive or negative, indicates whether the observation is larger than or smaller than the mean. The magnitude of the value reports how different (in the relevant numerical scale) an observation is from the mean.
Standard deviation	In probability theory and statistics, the Standard deviation of a statistical population, a data set, or a probability distribution is the square root of its variance. Standard deviation is a widely used measure of the variability or dispersion, being algebraically more tractable though practically less robust than the expected deviation or average absolute deviation.

Chapter 18. Statistical Quality Control

Chapter 18. Statistical Quality Control

It shows how much variation there is from the `average` (mean, or expected/budgeted value).

Random number table

A random number table has been used in statistics for tasks such as selected random samples. This was much more effective than manually selecting the random samples. Nowadays, tables of random numbers have been replaced by computational random number generators.

Binomial probability

Binomial probability typically deals with the probability of several successive decisions, each of which has two possible outcomes.

The probability of an event can be expressed as a Binomial probability if its outcomes can be broken down into two probabilities p and q, where p and q are complementary For example, tossing a coin can be either heads or tails, each which have a (theoretical) probability of 0.5. Rolling a four on a six-sided die can be expressed as the probability (1/6) of getting a 4 or the probability (5/6) of rolling something else.

If an event has a probability, p, of happening, then the probability of it happening twice is p^2, and in general p^n for n successive trials. If we want to know the probability of rolling a die three times and getting two fours and one other number (in that specific order) it becomes:

$$
\begin{aligned}
P(2 \text{ rolls of four and 1 other}) &= P(2 \text{ rolls of four})P(1 \text{ other}) \\
&= P(\text{rolls of four})^2 P(\text{other})^1 \\
&= (\tfrac{1}{6})^2(\tfrac{5}{6})^1 \\
&= 2.3\%
\end{aligned}
$$

Probability distribution

In probability theory and statistics, a Probability distribution identifies either the probability of each value of a random variable (when the variable is discrete), or the probability of the value falling within a particular interval (when the variable is continuous). The Probability distribution describes the range of possible values that a random variable can attain and the probability that the value of the random variable is within any (measurable) subset of that range.

When the random variable takes values in the set of real numbers, the Probability distribution is completely described by the cumulative distribution function, whose value at each real x is the probability that the random variable is smaller than or equal to x.

Chapter 18. Statistical Quality Control

Chapter 18. Statistical Quality Control

Continuous	In probability theory, a probability distribution is called continuous if its cumulative distribution function is continuous. This is equivalent to saying that for random variables X with the distribution in question, Pr[X = a] = 0 for all real numbers a, i.e.: the probability that X attains the value a is zero, for any number a. If the distribution of X is continuous then X is called a continuous random variable.
Normal distribution	In probability theory and statistics, the Normal distribution or Gaussian distribution is a continuous probability distribution that describes data that cluster around a mean or average. The graph of the associated probability density function is bell-shaped, with a peak at the mean, and is known as the Gaussian function or bell curve. The Gaussian distribution is one of many things named after Carl Friedrich Gauss, who used it to analyze astronomical data, and determined the formula for its probability density function.
Critical value	In differential topology, a Critical value of a differentiable function $f: M \to N$ between differentiable manifolds is the value $f(x) \in N$ of a critical point $x \in M$. The basic result on Critical values is Sard's lemma. The set of Critical values can be quite irregular; but in Morse theory it becomes important to consider real-valued functions on a manifold M, such that the set of Critical values is in fact finite.
Random sampling	In random sampling every combination of items from the frame, or stratum, has a known probability of occurring, but these probabilities are not necessarily equal. With any form of sampling there is a risk that the sample may not adequately represent the population but with random sampling there is a large body of statistical theory which quantifies the risk and thus enables an appropriate sample size to be chosen.
Systematic sample	A systematic sample is a statistical method involving the selection of a specific interval element from a sampling frame. Using this procedure each element in the population has a known and equal probability of selection. This makes it functionally similar to simple random sampling.
Student t distribution	The Student t distribution is a probability distribution that arises in the problem of estimating the mean of a normally distributed population when the sample size is small. It is the basis of the popular Student's t-tests for the statistical significance of the difference between two sample means, and for confidence intervals for the difference between two population means.

Chapter 18. Statistical Quality Control

Chapter 18. Statistical Quality Control

Dummy variable

In regression analysis, a Dummy variable is one that takes the values 0 or 1 to indicate the absence or presence of some categorical effect that may be expected to shift the outcome. For example, in econometric time series analysis, Dummy variables may be used to indicate the occurrence of wars, or major strikes. It could thus be thought of as a truth value represented as a numerical value 0 or 1.

Studentized range

In statistics, the Studentized range computed from a list $x_1, .. \, x_n$ of numbers is

$$\frac{\max\{\, x_1, \ldots, x_n \,\} - \min\{\, x_1, \ldots, x_n \,\}}{s},$$

where

$$s^2 = \frac{1}{n-1} \sum_{i=1}^{n} (x_i - \overline{x})^2,$$

is the sample variance and

$$\overline{x} = \frac{x_1 + \cdots + x_n}{n}$$

is the sample mean.

Generally, studentized means adjusted by dividing by an estimate of a population standard deviation.

Studentized range distribution

Studentized range distribution is the same regardless of the expected value and standard deviation of the normal distribution from which the sample is drawn. This probability distribution has applications to hypothesis testing and multiple comparisons.

Runs test

The Runs test is a non-parametric test that checks a randomness hypothesis for a two-valued data sequence. More precisely, it can be used to test the hypothesis that the elements of the sequence are mutually independent.

Chapter 18. Statistical Quality Control

Chapter 18. Statistical Quality Control

A `run` of a sequence is a maximal non-empty segment of the sequence consisting of adjacent equal elements. For example, the sequence `++++---+++--+++++++----` consists of six runs, three of which consist of +`s and the others of –`s. If +s and –s alternate randomly, the number of runs in a sequence of length N for which it is given that there are N_+ occurrences of + and N_- occurrences of - (so $N = N_+ + N_-$) is a random variable whose conditional distribution - given the observation of N_+ and N_- - is approximately normal with:

· mean
$$\mu = \frac{2 N_+ N_-}{N} + 1,$$

· variance
$$\sigma^2 = \frac{2 N_+ N_- (2 N_+ N_- - N)}{N^2 (N-1)} = \frac{(\mu - 1)(\mu - 2)}{N - 1}.$$

Mann-Whitney U test	In statistics, the Mann-Whitney U test is a non-parametric test for assessing whether two independent samples of observations come from the same distribution. It is one of the best-known non-parametric significance tests. It was proposed initially by Frank Wilcoxon in 1945, for equal sample sizes, and extended to arbitrary sample sizes and in other ways by H. B. Mann and Whitney (1947).
P-value	In statistical significance testing, the P-value is the probability of obtaining a test statistic at least as extreme as the one that was actually observed, assuming that the null hypothesis is true. A closely related concept is the E-value, which is the average number of times in multiple testing that one expects to obtain a test statistic at least as extreme as the one that was actually observed, assuming that the null hypothesis is true. When the tests are statistically independent the E-value is the product of the number of tests and the P-value.
Sample	In statistics, a Sample is a subset of a population. Typically, the population is very large, making a census or a complete enumeration of all the values in the population impractical or impossible. The Sample represents a subset of manageable size.
Probability sampling	Probability sampling is technique of sampling that uses som form of random selection. In order to have randon selection, there must be a set up process that assuraes that the different units in the population have equal probabilities of being chosen.

Chapter 18. Statistical Quality Control

CPSIA information can be obtained at www.ICGtesting.com
Printed in the USA
LVOW032150260212

270541LV00001B/85/P